EXECUTIV...
Mike Mif...
Sarah Gal...

MANAGING EDITOR
Natalie Earnheart

CREATIVE DIRECTOR
Christine Ricks

PHOTOGRAPHY TEAM
Mike Brunner, Lauren Dorton, Jennifer Dowling,
Dustin Weant

PATTERN TEAM
Edie McGinnis, Denise Lane, Jessica Woods,
Gregg Allnutt

PROJECT DESIGN TEAM
Jenny Doan, Natalie Earnheart, Janet Yamamoto

EDITOR & COPYWRITERS
Jenny Doan, Natalie Earnheart, Katie Mifsud,
Camille Maddox, Nichole Spravzoff, Edie McGinnis

SEWIST TEAM
Jenny Doan, Natalie Earnheart, Janet Yamamoto,
Carol Henderson, Denise Lane, Janice Richardson,
Jamey Stone

QUILTING & BINDING DEPARTMENT
Sarah Richardson, Betty Bates, Karla Zinkand, Natalie
Loucks, Debbie Elder, Jan Meek, Angela Wilson,
Chelsea White, Mary McPhee, Charlene McCabe,
Dennis Voss, Debbie Allen, Jamee Gilgour, Michelle
Templeton, Frank Jones, Kara Snow, Ethan Lucas,
Devin Ragle, Bruce VanIperen, Lyndia Lovell, Aaron
Crawford, Cyera Cottrill, Deborah Warner, Salena
Smiley, Francesca Flemming, Rachael Joyce, Bernice
Kelly, Deloris Burnett

LOCATION CREDIT
Mari's House Bed and Breakfast
200 East School Street
Hamilton, Mo. 64644

Morning Star Cottage
411 South Davis,
Hamilton, Mo. 64644

Peggy and Robert Adams home

PRINTING COORDINATORS
Rob Stoebener, Seann Dwyer

PRINTING SERVICES
Walsworth Print Group
803 South Missouri
Marceline, MO 64658

CONTACT US
Missouri Star Quilt Company
114 N Davis
Hamilton, Mo. 64644
888-571-1122
info@missouriquiltco.com

content

Oops! Sometimes we make mistakes.
To find corrections to every issue of Block
go to: **www.msqc.co/corrections**

hello
from MSQC

I recall not too long ago hearing the forecast on Groundhog's Day that there would be six more weeks of winter. I don't necessarily believe that a furry, little animal can tell the weather, but this certainly felt like a longer winter than last year—and thankfully, it's over! I suppose it always seems that way when I'm in the middle of it. The long, gray days can wear on me, but when I step into my quilting room, the gray melts away and I feel like I'm bathed in sunshine.

Sitting down to sew is like a mini vacation. Even though I quilt for a living, I still thoroughly enjoy the process of making something beautiful and useful. It gives me energy to keep going through the less exciting moments in life. And that's exactly what creativity can do for us!

There's nothing like an armful of bright, colorful fabric to chase the blues away! Even if I'm not sure what I want to make, I start looking through my stash and some thing's bound to catch my eye. So, the next time you're feeling less than inspired, pick yourself up, pull out some pretty fabrics, and just see where they take you. Let the joy of quilting fill your heart no matter what the weather's like outside.

JENNY DOAN
MISSOURI STAR QUILT CO

TRY OUR APP

It's easy to keep up on every issue of BLOCK magazine. Access it from all your devices. And when you subscribe to BLOCK, it's free with your subscription! For the app search BLOCK magazine in the app store. Available for both Apple and Android.

4x4 quilt

Spring cleaning. These two simple words might fill you with excitement to scrub and dust and organize every little thing in your house, or they might fill you with a heavy sense of dread. Overall, my home is clean, but a comfortable kind of clutter has built up over the years. I don't usually get rid of things anymore, I just keep buying new containers to store it all in! A good friend told me that my house is exactly like you would expect it to be. It's warm and homey, with quilts all over the place. I love that. Just don't go opening any drawers around here!

Many of you are collectors, like me. I find that quilters especially tend to love neat old antiques and we can't ever get rid of those fabric scraps because you never know when they might come in handy. I totally, completely understand. With the new trend toward minimalism, I find myself somewhat resistant to change. I like the idea, but not completely. I don't want to get rid of those things that make me smile, but I am also a bit tired of drowning in stuff. I know I need to let go of some things, but what?

There are so many opinions about organization, but there are no hard and fast rules in my book. It's personal. It's up to you. Whether you tend to be a minimalist or a maximalist, visualize

For the tutorial and everything you need to make this quilt visit:
www.msqc.co/blockspring18

the kind of space you'd like to live in and do what you can to make that happen. I like that I live in a cozy house filled with quilts. I'd never trade that in for a white-walled room without the warm glow of a fireplace. But that's me.

As you may know, I'm a big fan of Mary Poppins. I'd love it if she came to my house and started snapping her fingers. And she's right about one thing, "In every job that must be done,

there is an element of fun." I try to remember that when I go about decluttering. There is a reward in this arduous task. When I'm through, I'll have a more enjoyable workspace. I'll be able to find things easier. I can give away things I'm no longer using. It's all positive. The trick is to get started! Let's go for it, shall we?

materials

QUILT SIZE
70" x 78" finished

BLOCK SIZE
8" finished

QUILT TOP
1 roll of 2½" print strips
1¾ yards background – includes
inner border

OUTER BORDER
1¼ yards

BINDING
¾ yard

BACKING
5 yards - vertical seam(s)

SAMPLE QUILT
Longitude Batiks by Kate Spain for
Moda Fabrics

1 cut

From the background fabric, cut:

- (7) 4½" strips across the width of the fabric – subcut each strip into 4½" squares. Each strip will yield 8 squares and a **total of 56** are needed.

- (4) 2½" strips across the width of the fabric. Set aside the remainder of the fabric for the inner border.

2 sew

For this quilt, we will be making 2 separate blocks and alternating them as we lay out the quilt and sew the rows together.

3 block a – 16-patch

Make a strip set by sewing 2 contrasting 2½" print strips together lengthwise with right sides facing. Open and press the seam allowance toward the darker fabric. **Make 14 strip sets** and cut each into (8) 5" increments. **3A**

Mix up the 5" pieces and sew 8 into a row. Alternate the lighter squares with darker squares to make a pieced strip. **Make 14.** **3B**

Fold over the first block of the strip. Measure 2½" from the outer edge of the seam line and cut. You will have (1) 2-patch and (1)

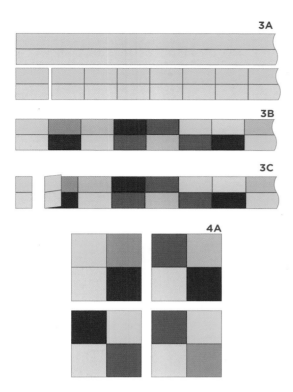

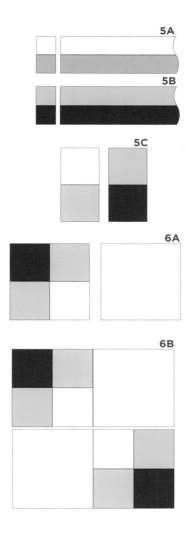

4-patch. Continue folding and cutting to make 4-patches. When you reach the end of the strip, you will have enough fabric left to cut 1 more 2-patch. Sew the (2) 2-patches together to make a 4-patch. Each strip will yield (8) 4-patch units and you need a **total of 112. 3C**

4 block construction

Select (4) 4-patch units. Sew them together into a 4-patch formation as shown to make a 16-patch block.

Make 28 and set aside for the moment. **4A**

Block size: 8″ finished.

5 block b

Sew a background 2½″ strip to a print 2½″ strip along the length with right sides facing. Open each and press the seam allowance

toward the darker fabric. **Make 4** and cut each strip set into 2½″ increments to make 2-patch units. Each strip set will yield 16 and a **total of 56** are needed. **5A**

Sew a 2½″ print strip to a contrasting 2½″ print strip along the length with right sides facing.

Open each and press the seam allowance toward the darker fabric. **Make 4** and cut each strip set into 2½″ increments to make 2-patch units. Each strip set will yield 16 and a **total of 56** are needed. **5B**

Sew a print/print 2-patch unit to a background/print 2-patch unit together as shown to make a 4-patch. **Make 56. 5C**

6 block construction

Sew a 4-patch unit to a 4½″ background square. **Make 2. 6A**

Sew the 2 sections together into a 4-patch formation as shown to complete the block. **Make 28. 6B**

Block size: 8″ finished.

7 arrange and sew

Lay out the blocks in rows. Each row is made up of 7 blocks and 8 rows are needed. Block A and Block B alternate. Refer to the

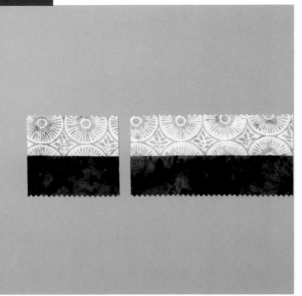

1   Make a strip set by sewing 2 contrasting 2½" prints strips together lengthwise with right sides facing. Make 14 and cut each into (8) 5" increments.

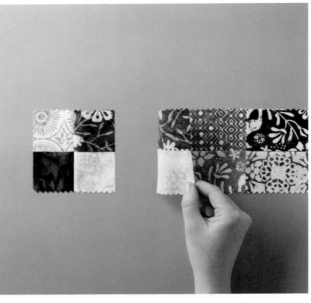

2   Mix up the 5" strip-set pieces and sew them together into a long strip. Fold over the first block of the strip. Measure 2½" from the outer edge of the seam line and cut. You will have (1) 2-patch and (1) 4-patch. Continue folding and cutting until you reach the end of the strip.

3   Sew (4) 4-patch units together to complete 1 A Block. Make 28.

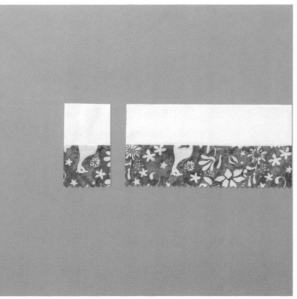
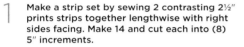

4   Make a strip set by sewing a 2½" background strip to a 2½" print strip lengthwise with right sides facing. Make 4 and cut each strip set into 2½" increments to make (16) 2-patch units

5   Sew 2 contrasting print strips together lengthwise with right sides facing to make another strip set. Make 4 and cut each strip set into 2½" increments to make (16) 2-patch units.

6   Sew a print/print 2-patch unit to a background/print 2-patch unit to make a 4-patch. Make (2) 4-patches per block and sew each to a 4½" background square as shown to complete 1 B Block. Make 28.

diagram to the right. Notice that beginning with Row 5, the blocks alternate differently. After the blocks have been sewn into rows, press the seam allowances of the odd-numbered rows toward the right and the even-numbered rows toward the left to make the seams "nest."

Sew the rows together to complete the center of the quilt.

8 inner border

Cut (7) 2½" strips across the width of the fabric. Sew the strips together end-to-end to make one long strip. Trim the borders from this strip.

Refer to Borders (pg. 102) in the Construction Basics to measure and cut the inner borders. The strips are approximately 64½" for the sides and approximately 60½" for the top and bottom.

9 outer border

Cut (7) 5½" strips across the width of the fabric. Sew the strips together end-to-end to make one long strip. Trim the borders from this strip.

Refer to Borders (pg. 102) in the Construction Basics to measure and cut the outer borders. The strips are approximately 68½" for the sides and approximately 70½" for the top and bottom.

10 quilt and bind

Layer the quilt with batting and backing and quilt. After the quilting is complete, square up the quilt and trim away all excess batting and backing. Add binding to complete the quilt. See Construction Basics (pg. 102) for binding instructions.

For the tutorial and everything
you need to make this quilt visit:
www.msqc.co/blockspring18

bordered
nine-patch

When the bare branches of the trees start to form tiny buds and new growth pushes up through the dark earth, it thrills me. I always know spring is coming when the birds start singing. Every time I'm out on a walk, I watch for birds and try to spy where their nests are hidden among the trees. The melody of their chirping is everywhere and I adore that sweet sound. Everything outside smells and feels new and fresh. It makes me want to throw open the windows and soak it all in. Spring feels like a new start. I like to think of it as a yearly do over! You can always begin again and there is hope in new beginnings.

To celebrate the arrival of spring, this year I got hyacinth plants for myself and all my girls. My mom and I both love poetry and she would often quote the poem by John Greenleaf Whittier that says:

> If thou of fortune be bereft,
> And in thy store there be but left
> Two loaves—sell one, and with the dole
> Buy hyacinths to feed thy soul.

bordered nine-patch quilt

As I took each daughter their first plant of spring and quoted this poem to them, it warmed my soul.

After a monochromatic winter with little color in the landscape, seeing so much greenery growing around me is energizing and inspiring. Green is the color of spring! I honestly believe that nowhere else in the world gets as green as the Midwest. It's so vibrant, it's practically neon. I love all the colors of spring—from our Redbud tree, with all its cute, pink blossoms to the yellow Forsythia that bursts

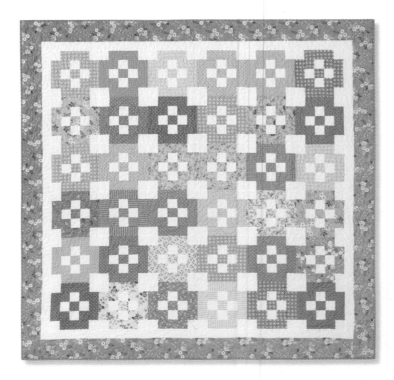

with bright yellow blooms before it even gets leaves. The signs of spring wake me up to the world all around me, bring me out of hibernation, and help me pause to consider all the wonderful things that make life hopeful. They say the only thing that is constant is change, and whether it is highly anticipated or unexpected, change certainly does come for all of us. Each spring is a reminder that change can be pleasant, even welcome.

materials

QUILT SIZE
73" x 73"

BLOCK SIZE
10" finished

QUILT TOP
1 roll of 2½" print strips
1¾ yards background fabric – includes
inner border

OUTER BORDER
1¼ yards

BINDING
¾ yard

BACKING
4½ yards - vertical seam(s)

SAMPLE QUILT
Nest by Lella Boutique for Moda Fabrics

1 cut

From each of (36) 2½" print strips,
cut:

- (5) 2½" squares,

- (4) 2½" x 6½" rectangles.

Stack all matching prints together.

From the background fabric, cut:

- (25) 2½" strips across the
  width of the fabric – subcut 18
  strips into 2½" squares. Each
  strip will yield 16 squares and a
  total of 288 are needed. Set
  aside the remaining 7 strips for
  the inner border.

2 block construction

Pick up a stack of matching print
pieces. **Make a 9-patch** by sewing
a 2½" print square to either side of
a 2½" background square. **Make 2
rows** in this manner. **2A**

2A

2B

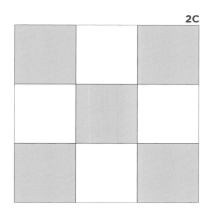

2C

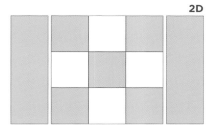

2D

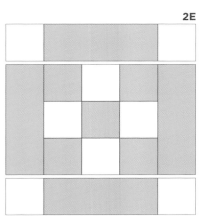

2E

Sew a 2½" background square to either side of a 2½" print square. **2B**

Sew the 3 rows together to complete the center 9-patch. **2C**

Sew a 2½" x 6½" rectangle to 2 sides of the 9-patch. **2D**

Stitch a 2½" background square to each end of the remaining (2) 2½" x 6½" print rectangles in the stack. Sew 1 to the top of the block and 1 to the bottom to complete the block. **Make 36**. **2E**

Block Size: 10" finished.

3 arrange and sew

Lay out the blocks in rows. Each row is made up of 6 blocks and 6 rows are needed. After sewing each row together, press the seam allowances of the odd rows toward the right and the even rows toward the left to make the seam allowances "nest." Sew the rows together to complete the center of the quilt.

4 inner border

Pick up the (7) 2½" background strips that were cut earlier. Sew the strips together end-to-end to make one long strip. Trim the borders from this strip.

Refer to Borders (pg. 102) in the Construction Basics to measure and cut the inner borders. The strips are approximately 60½" for the sides and approximately 64½" for the top and bottom.

5 outer border

Cut (8) 5" strips across the width of the fabric. Sew the strips together end-to-end to make one long strip. Trim the borders from this strip.

Refer to Borders (pg. 102) in the Construction Basics to measure and cut the outer borders. The strips are approximately 64½" for the sides and approximately 73½" for the top and bottom.

6 quilt and bind

Layer the quilt with batting and backing and quilt. After the quilting is complete, square up the quilt and trim away all excess batting and backing. Add binding to complete the quilt. See Construction Basics (pg. 102) for binding instructions.

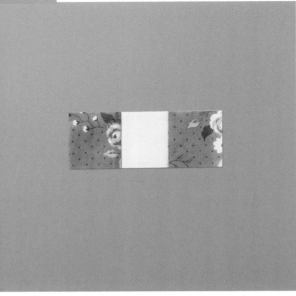

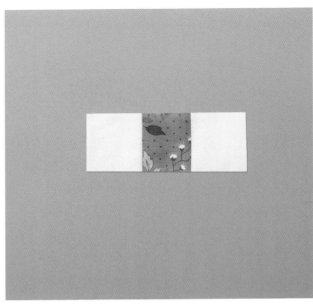

1 Sew a 2½″ print square to either side of a 2½″ background square. Make 2 rows like this.

2 Sew a 2½″ background square to either side of a 2½″ print square. Make 1 row like this.

3 Stitch the 3 rows together to make a 9-patch block.

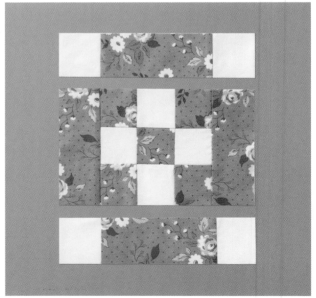

4 Sew a 2½″ x 6½″ rectangle to 2 sides of the 9-patch block.

5 Sew a 2½″ background square to each end of the remaining 2½″ x 6½″ print rectangles in the stack. Sew 1 to the top and 1 to the bottom to complete the block.

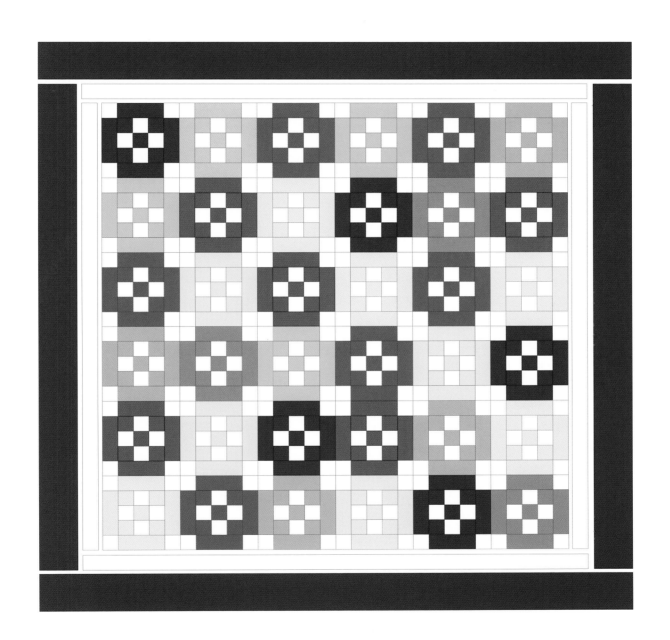

card trick

As a child growing up in Spreckels, California, our Easter egg hunt would often take place at the beach. The Marina State Beach park was just 20 minutes down the road and we visited often. Hiding plastic eggs filled with tempting candies wasn't such a great idea with all those sneaky seagulls, occasional blowing sand, and unexpected waves washing up on shore. But my mother was an ingenious woman and she would hide little, decorated paper eggs in the seagrass growing in thick patches throughout the dunes. She carefully labeled each with a code like "MB", which meant it could be traded in for a "marshmallow bunny" when we got back home. I loved that tradition and now Ron and I continue it with our grandchildren. It saves us the hassle of stuffing endless plastic eggs, plus, you won't find a forgotten plastic egg months later in the garden, crawling with ants.

For the tutorial and everything you need to make this quilt visit:
www.msqc.co/blockspring18

On Easter Sunday, we always have dinner together as a family. There's nothing like a big plate of ham, potatoes, jello salad, and buttery rolls to get you in the mood for some fast and furious Easter egg hunting! After dinner, the kids go upstairs to wait while the rest of us hide the paper eggs all over the yard. Eagerly awaiting their chance to go hunting, the children keep peeking out the door, trying to catch a glimpse of where the eggs might be hidden.

Finally, the long-awaited moment arrives and the kids burst forth into the backyard, looking for eggs! They could be hidden just about anywhere: between the slats of the fence, in tall bunches of flowers, tucked deep inside overgrown bushes, in the branches of trees, under rocks, you name it. My children have become very clever with their hiding places and their own kids are getting pretty good at finding them!

When it's all said and done, and the candies have been handed out, I sit back with a smile on my face. I enjoy the playful chatter around me and a chocolate bunny or two, and I let the joy of this hopeful season fill me with peace.

materials

QUILT SIZE
82½" x 93¾"

BLOCK SIZE
11¼" finished

QUILT TOP
1 roll of 2½" print strips
4¾ yards background fabric –
includes inner border

OUTER BORDER
1¾ yards

BINDING
¾ yard

BACKING
8½ yards - vertical seam(s)
or 2¾ yards - 108" wide

SAMPLE QUILT
Monday, Monday by Jill Finley of
Penny Rose Fabrics for Riley Blake
Designs

1 cut

From the background fabric, cut:

- (17) 7" strips across the width of
  the fabric - subcut each strip
  into 7" squares. Each strip will
  yield 5 squares and a **total of 84**
  are needed.

- (11) 2½" strips across the width
  of the fabric – subcut each strip
  into 2½" squares. Each strip
  will yield 16 squares and a **total
  of 168** are needed.

Set aside the remaining
background fabric for the inner
border.

Select 28 print 2½" strips. From
each, cut:

- (6) 4½" rectangles
- (6) 2½" squares

Stack all matching print pieces
together.

Select 11 print 2½" strips, cut
each into (16) 2½" squares for a
total of 168. Set aside to use for
snowballing the corners of each
block.

2 block construction

Pair a 4½" rectangle with a
matching 2½" square to make

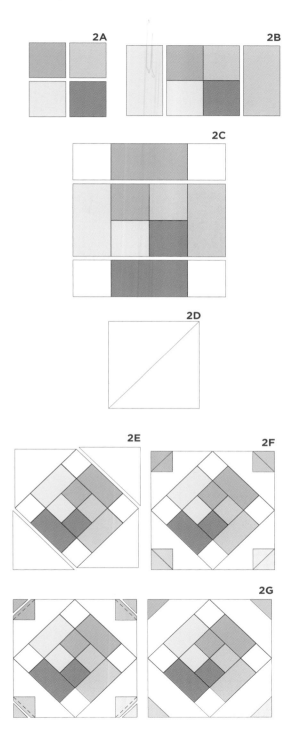

2A

2B

2C

2D

2E

2F

2G

1 set, a **total of 4 sets** are needed for each block.

Sew the (4) 2½" print squares together into a 4-patch. **2A**

Add a 4½" rectangle to either side of the 4-patch, making sure a rectangle is touching a matching square. **2B**

Sew a 2½" background square to both ends of the remaining 2 rectangles. Sew one to the top and one to the bottom of the 4-patch, again making sure the rectangle you are sewing in place matches the square in the 4-patch it touches. **2C**

Select (2) 7" background squares. Cut each from corner to corner once on the diagonal. **2D**

Sew a background triangle to 2 opposing sides of the bordered 4-patch. Add a background triangle to the remaining 2 sides. **2E**

Square the blocks to 11¾" before snowballing the corners.

Mark a line on the diagonal on the reverse side of (4) 2½" print squares. Place a marked square on each corner of the block with right sides facing. **2F**

Sew on the marked line, then trim ¼" from the sewn seam. Press the seam allowance toward the darker fabric to complete the block. **Make 42**. **2G**

Block size: 11¼" finished

3 arrange and sew

Lay out the blocks in rows. Each row is made up of 6 blocks and 7 rows are needed. After the blocks have been sewn into rows, press the seam allowances of the odd-numbered rows toward the right and the even-numbered rows toward the left to make the seams "nest."

Sew the rows together to complete the center of the quilt.

4 inner border

Cut (8) 2½" strips across the width of the fabric. Sew the strips together end-to-end to make one long strip. Trim the borders from this strip.

Refer to Borders (pg. 102) in the Construction Basics to measure and cut the inner borders. The strips are approximately 79¼" for the sides and approximately 72" for the top and bottom.

5 outer border

Cut (9) 6" strips across the width of the fabric. Sew the strips together end-to-end to make one long strip. Trim the borders from this strip.

Refer to Borders (pg. 102) in the Construction Basics to measure and cut the outer borders. The strips are

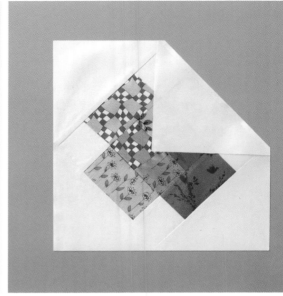

1 Sew (4) 2½″ print squares together to make a 4-patch. Add a 4½″ rectangle to either side of the 4-patch, making sure the rectangles touch a matching square.

2 Sew a 2½″ background square to each end of the remaining 2 rectangles. Sew 1 to the top of the 4-patch and 1 to the bottom, again making sure the rectangle you are sewing in place matches the square in the 4-patch it touches.

3 After cutting 2 background 7″ squares from corner to corner once on the diagonal, sew a triangle to opposing sides of the bordered 4-patch. Add a background triangle to the 2 remaining sides.

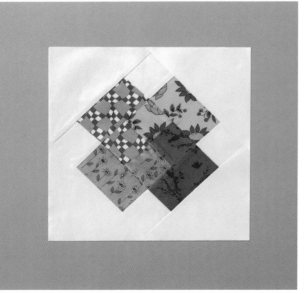

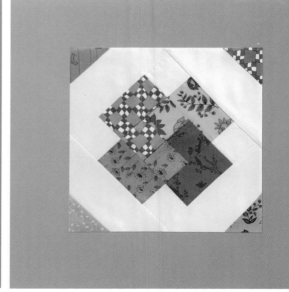

4 Press the block and square to 11¾″.

5 Mark a line from corner to corner once on the diagonal on the reverse side of (4) 2½″ print squares. Place each on one corner of the block and sew on the marked line. Trim ¼″ away from the sewn seam.

6 Open the snowballed corners and press the seam allowances toward the darker fabric to complete the block.

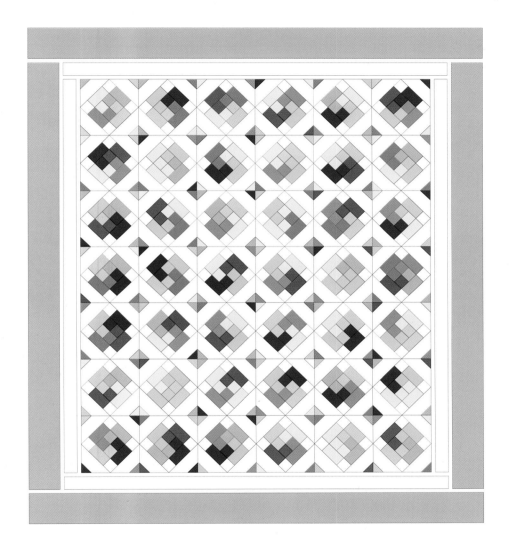

approximately 83¼" for the sides and approximately 83" for the top and bottom.

6 quilt and bind

Layer the quilt with batting and backing and quilt. After the quilting is complete, square up the quilt and trim away all excess batting and backing. Add binding to complete the quilt. See Construction Basics (pg. 102) for binding instructions.

crown
quilt

Spring is a time of new beginnings. We clean out clutter and trade old habits for new ones. It's a chance to start fresh with the hope of being a little bit better each day.

Of course, if you set your sights on running a marathon or writing the next great American novel, you may be disappointed in your progress. Gigantic goals are practically doomed to fail, unless you have a massive amount of fortitude and the discipline to make it happen. Instead, consider starting small with itty bitty baby goals. Choose things that are uplifting and simple. Things that will make you—and everyone around you—just a little bit happier. Here are a few things I've tried.

Set a daily alarm for nine o'clock in the morning. When it goes off, stop what you are doing and send a cheerful text to a friend. Your words of encouragement or gratitude will brighten their morning and set the tone for a optimistic day.

"Hide" your tv remote underneath your journal. Before you turn on the evening news, take a moment to jot down a few highlights from the day. You'll be more likely to recognize the good in even ordinary days, and the holidays, you'll have a lovely record of the year.

For the tutorial and everything you need to make this quilt visit:
www.msqc.co/blockspring18

crown quilt

Drink more water. Treat yourself to a cute, new water bottle, and keep it close at hand. Proper hydration is so good for your body. It reduces headaches and crankiness, improves digestion and energy levels, and can even make your skin glow!

Pick up a cardboard box and take a stroll through the house. Any time you walk past something you no longer use—ill fitting clothing, toys no one plays with, books you've read once and won't read again—place it in the box. But be careful, when the box is full, don't set it down! March right out to your car and drive to the local thrift shop. Donate your items and never look back! Repeat as often as you wish for a delightfully uncluttered home.

Claim thirty minutes of every day as your very own. Take a quiet stroll through the park. Sneak off to the local bakery for a warm sweet roll. Close the door to your sewing room to sew your heart out. Whatever you choose to do, you'll emerge refreshed and better able to face the challenges of the day.

This spring, I encourage you to take a moment to set a goal or two—something small, something pleasant—and make it happen! And let this be the year that working on your goals finally becomes fun!

materials

QUILT SIZE
88" X 88" finished

BLOCK SIZE
24" finished

QUILT TOP
3 packages 5" print squares
3 packages 5" white squares
2 yards contrasting fabric (we used black)

INNER BORDER
¾ yards

OUTER BORDER
1¾ yards

BINDING
¾ yard

BACKING
8 yards - vertical seam(s) or
2¾ yards - 108" wide.

SAMPLE QUILT
Mark to Make by Malka Dubrawsky for Robert Kaufman

1 cut

From the black fabric, cut:

- (3) 8½" strips across the width of the fabric – subcut each strip into 8½" squares. Each strip will yield 4 squares and a **total of 9** are needed. Subcut the remaining 8½" x 31½" piece into (4) 4½" squares and set aside for the moment.

- (5) 5" strips across the width of the fabric – subcut each strip into 5" squares. Each strip will yield 8 squares and a **total of 36** are needed.

- (4) 4½" strips across the width of the fabric – subcut each strip into 4½" squares. Each strip will yield 8 squares and a **total of 36** are needed. Add the 4½" squares cut previously to the stack in order to have enough pieces.

2 make half-square triangles

On the reverse side of 108 white 5" squares, draw a line from corner to corner once on the diagonal. **2A**

Layer 36 white 5" squares with 36 black 5" squares with right sides facing. Sew ¼" on both sides of the line. Cut on the drawn line, open to reveal 2 half-square triangle units. Press the seam allowances toward the darker fabric. Each sewn set of squares will yield 2 half-square triangle units and you need a **total of 72**. Square each to 4½". **2B**

Layer each of the remaining marked white 5" squares (72) with a 5" print square with right sides facing. Again, sew on both sides of the drawn line. Cut on the drawn line, open to reveal 2 half-square triangle units. Press the seam allowance to the darker fabric. You will have a **total of 144** half-square triangle units. Square each to 4½". See diagram **2B**.

3 trim

Choose (36) 5" squares from the remaining prints. Trim each square to 4½".

4 block construction

Sew a 4½" black square to a black/white half-square triangle unit. Add a print/white half-square triangle, then another. Follow with a black/white half-square triangle and end the row with a black square. Be aware of how the half-square triangles are oriented. **Make 2 rows** like this. **4A**

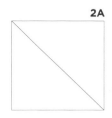

2A

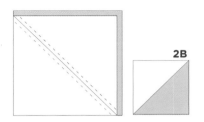

2B

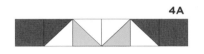

4A

4B

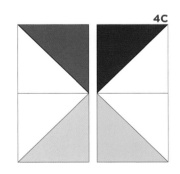

4C

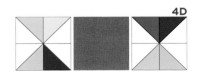

4D

Sew a black/white half-square triangle unit to a 4½" print square. Add a print/white half-square triangle, then another. Follow with a print 4½" square and end the row with a black/white half-square triangle. Again, be aware of how the half-square triangles are oriented. **Make 2 rows** like this. **4B**

Sew 2 print/white half-square triangles together into a flying geese unit. **Make 4** and sew them together into pairs as shown. **4C**

Sew the paired flying geese to either side of an 8½" black square. **4D**

Sew the rows you have made together to complete the block. **Make 9. 4E**

Block Size: 24" finished

5 arrange and sew

Lay out the blocks in 3 rows of 3. Press the seam allowances of the first and third rows toward the right and the seam allowances of the center row toward the left to make the seams "nest." After pressing, sew the rows together.

6 inner border

Cut (8) 2½" strips across the width of the fabric. Sew the strips together end-to-end to make one

4E

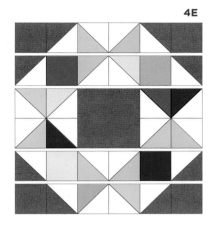

long strip. Trim the borders from this strip.

Refer to Borders (pg. 102) in the Construction Basics to measure and cut the inner borders. The strips are approximately 72½" for the sides and approximately 76½" for the top and bottom.

7 outer border

Cut (9) 6½" strips across the width of the fabric. Sew the strips together end-to-end to make one long strip. Trim the borders from this strip.

Refer to Borders (pg. 102) in the Construction Basics to measure and cut the outer borders. The strips are approximately 76½" for the sides and approximately 88½" for the top and bottom.

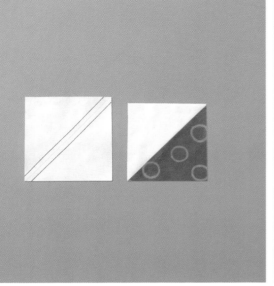

1 Draw a line from corner to corner once on the diagonal on the reverse side of 108 white 5″ squares. Layer a white square with a print square and sew on both sides of the drawn line using a ¼″ seam allowance. Cut on the drawn line and open each side to reveal a half-square triangle unit.

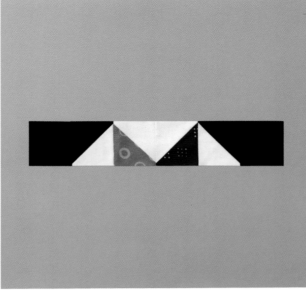

2 Sew a 4½″ black square to a black/white half-square triangle unit. Add a print/white half-square triangle, then another. Follow with a black/white half-square triangle and end the row with a black square. Make 2 rows.

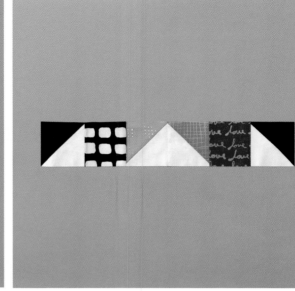

3 Sew a black/white half-square triangle unit to a 4½″ print square. Add a print/white half-square triangle, then another. Follow with a print 4½″ square and end the row with a black/white half-square triangle. Make 2 rows.

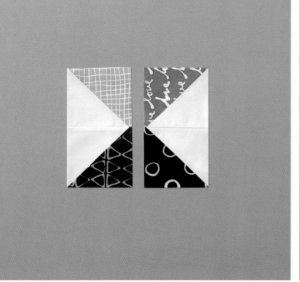

4 Sew 2 print/white half-square triangles together into flying geese units. Make 4 and sew them together into pairs as shown.

5 Sew the paired flying geese to either side of an 8½″ black square to make the center row.

6 Sew the rows together as shown to complete the block.

8 quilt and bind

Layer the quilt with batting and backing and quilt. After the quilting is complete, square up the quilt and trim away all excess batting and backing. Add binding to complete the quilt. See Construction Basics (pg. 102) for binding instructions.

disappearing pinwheel basket

Winter has a beauty all its own, but after months of ice-cold days, I start searching for the first signs of spring. They come slowly at first: the constant drip of thawing ice, a patch of purple crocus blooms, an early morning songbird. Before you know it, the earth is practically bursting with life. Flaming yellow forsythias, stately hyacinths, and fields of cheerful daffodils fill the landscape with color.

My favorite spring day is Lilac Day. That's the day I wake up and find my lilac tree covered in fragrant, purple blooms. I spend the morning gathering buckets full of blossoms, which I arrange into bouquets in mason jars. That afternoon, I load up the car to deliver flowers to the kids. Of course, the moment my children see me coming up the walk with a jar of blooms, they know: It's Lilac Day!

For the tutorial and everything
you need to make this quilt visit:
www.msqc.co/blockspring18

When the weather is nice, I spend as much time in my garden as I do in the sewing studio. I have quite a green thumb, and for many years I kept an enormous garden that produced mountains of flowers and plenty of food for our family of nine. At harvest time we feasted on sun-ripened tomatoes, fresh cucumbers, and juicy corn on the cob. We baked pies with the fruit from our trees. We carved jack-o'-lanterns out of homegrown pumpkins, and our table was always adorned with fresh cut flowers. That garden added such richness to our lives, and I absolutely adored it. To this day, I find great satisfaction working in dirt up to my elbows. To plant a seed and watch it grow to fruition is nothing short of magical.

Now that the children have families of their own, I keep a much smaller garden, but I still love my flowers. I keep quite a variety of plants, many of them in pots on my front porch. During the warmer months, that porch is like an extension of my house. We spend hours out there just soaking in the beauty of the great outdoors.

At the end of the year, when the weather gets too chilly for my potted plants, I carry them inside to find a winter home for each. A bookshelf, a window sill, my dining room credenza. Every available flat surface is outfitted with an arrangement of pots. By the time I am finished, the dining room looks like a rain forest. Never mind the fact that we have to eat among vines and blooms all winter, my plants are safe and cozy. But the moment the sun comes out to stay, I carry my flowers back out into the fresh air to welcome spring!

materials

QUILT SIZE
78" x 78"

BLOCK SIZE
11" finished

QUILT TOP
1 package 10" print squares
1 package of 10" background
squares

OUTER BORDER
1½ yards

BINDING
¾ yard

BACKING
7¼ yards - vertical seam(s)
or 2½ yards - 108" wide

SAMPLE QUILT
Roaring Twenties by Snow Leopard
Designs for Free Spirit Fabrics

1 sew

Make Half-Square Triangles

Layer a 10" print square with a 10" background square with right sides facing. Sew all the way around the outside edge using a ¼" seam allowance. Cut the sewn squares from corner to corner twice on the diagonal. Open and press the seam allowance toward the darker fabric. Each set will yield 4 half-square triangles. You need a **total of 168** half-square triangles or **42 sets**. Trim each half-square triangle to 6½". **1A**

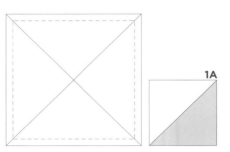

1A

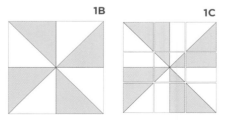

1B 1C

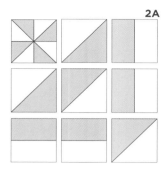

2A

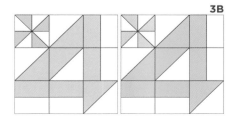

2B

Sew 4 half-square triangles together to make a pinwheel. **1B**

Measure the sewn block. Divide the measurement by 3 so the block can be cut into thirds. It should be about 4⅛″. Divide that number in half if you would like to use the center seam as a guide. Measure out 2¹⁄₁₆″ inches (or half of your measurement) and cut on either side of the center seam horizontally and vertically. **1C**

2 rearrange

Rearrange the pieces as shown into 3 rows of 3. **2A**

Before sewing anything together, lay out another block in the same manner. **2B**

3 trade

Trade the corner pinwheel in the first block with the corner pinwheel in the second. **3A**

Sew the pieces together into rows. Then sew the rows together to complete the block. **3B**

Always lay out 2 blocks at a time to make switching the pinwheels easier. **Make 36 blocks**.

Block size: 11″ finished

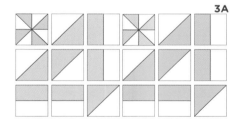

3A

3B

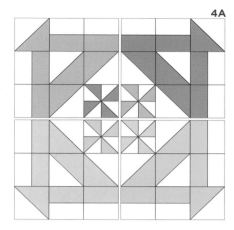

4A

4 lay out blocks

Group 4 basket blocks together with the pinwheel corners touching. Sewing the 4 together will make it easier to keep track of the blocks that had the pinwheels switched. **4A**

When you are happy with the way the quilt is laid out, sew the blocks together. Refer to the diagram on page 45.

5 border

Cut (8) 6½″ strips across the width of the fabric. Sew the strips together end-to-end to make one long strip. Trim the borders from this strip.

Refer to Borders (pg. 102) in the Construction Basics to measure and cut the outer borders. The strips are approximately 66½″ for the sides and approximately 78½″ for the top and bottom.

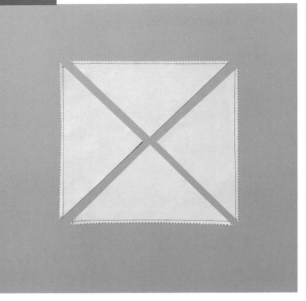

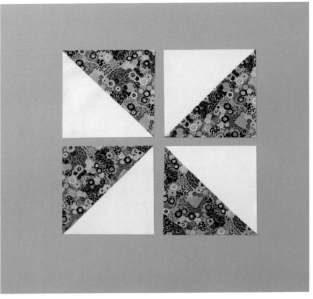

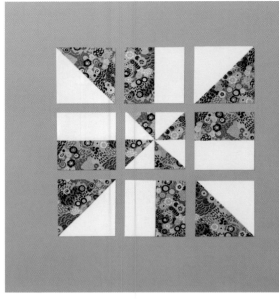

1 Layer a 10″ background square with a 10″ print square with right sides facing. Sew around the outside edge using a ¼″ seam allowance. Cut the sewn squares from corner to corner twice on the diagonal. Open to reveal 4 half-square triangle units.

2 Arrange the half-square triangles into a pinwheel formation and stitch them together.

3 Measure the sewn block and divide the measurement by 3. If you would like to use the center seam as a guide, measure out 2¹⁄₁₆″ (or half your measurement) and cut on either side of the center seam horizontally and vertically.

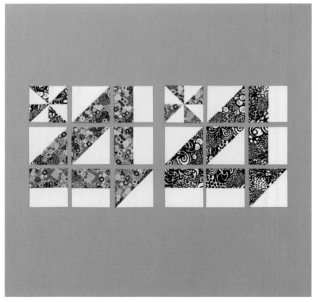

4 Rearrange the pieces as shown into 3 rows of 3. Wait to sew the rows together until you have laid out another block.

5 Lay out another block in the same manner. Trade the corner pinwheel in the first block with the corner pinwheel in the second. Sew the rows together.

6 quilt and bind

Layer the quilt with batting and backing and quilt. After the quilting is complete, square up the quilt and trim away all excess batting and backing. Add binding to complete the quilt. See Construction Basics (pg. 102) for binding instructions.

half & half

When the children were young, we lived in California where the weather was mild and pleasant. We did not experience the four seasons like we do in Missouri, but I loved the spring flowers. Every March we drove through the hills around Monterey and Carmel Valley in search of wild poppies and lupines.

Now that I live in Missouri, however, spring means a bit more than flowers. Winters can be long and hard, so when the days finally start to warm up, I can't help but get excited. The minute the earth starts to thaw and bloom, I am ready to go with my gardening gloves and trowel.

I love to visit our local Amish greenhouses to pick out plants for all my flower pots. The trees around town burst into bloom, and everywhere I go the air is filled with the wonderful aroma of new life.

For the tutorial and everything you need to make this quilt visit:
www.msqc.co/blockspring18

Living in such a rural community, we also get to enjoy all the newborn farm animals. This time of year, the brilliantly green fields of Caldwell County are filled with baby cows, goats, horses, and pigs.

But perhaps my favorite thing about spring is how we all come out of hibernation. All during winter we seem to scurry from home to work to the grocery store, always rushing to get out of the cold, and rarely pausing to chat. When the weather gets nice, and everyone steps outside to enjoy the sun, it's so nice to visit with the neighbors.

The town comes alive with the hustle and bustle of little league and farmers markets, and quilters from around the world start to arrive for a spring adventure filled with fabric. The weather is so nice, they can just stroll from one shop to the next without breaking a sweat!

When spring arrives, it's like waking up from a long winter's nap feeling energized and ready to take on the world. As the late comedian Robin Williams said, "Spring is nature's way of saying, 'Let's party!'"

materials

QUILT SIZE
77″ X 77″

BLOCK SIZE
11″ finished

QUILT TOP
1 package 10″ print squares
1 package 10″ background squares

INNER BORDER
¾ yard

OUTER BORDER
1 yard

BINDING
¾ yard

BACKING
4¾ yards - vertical seam(s)

SAMPLE QUILT
Sequoia by Edyta Sitar of Laundry
Basket Quilts for Andover Fabrics

1 sew

Layer a print 10″ square with a
background 10″ square. Sew all the way
around the outer edge using a ¼″ seam
allowance. Cut the sewn squares from
corner to corner twice on the diagonal.
Open to reveal 4 half-square triangle
units. Press the seam allowance toward
the darker fabric and square each
half-square triangle to 6½″. Stack all
matching half-square triangles together.
1A

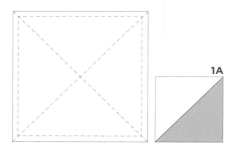

2 block a construction

Select 4 matching half-square
triangles. Cut each in half vertically and
horizontally. **2A**

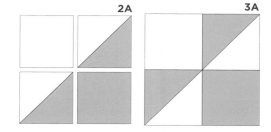

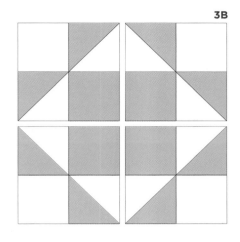

3B

3 rearrange

Rearrange the pieces into quadrants as shown. **Make 4** quadrants using the matching prints. **3A**

Sew the 4 quadrants together to complete Block A. **Make 18. 3B**

4 block b construction

Select 4 matching half-square triangles. Cut each in half vertically and horizontally. **4A**

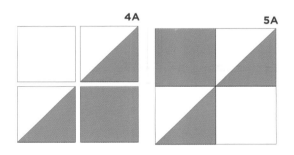

4A
5A

5 rearrange

Rearrange the pieces into quadrants as shown. **Make 4** quadrants using the matching prints. **5A**

Sew the 4 quadrants together to complete Block B. **Make 18 5B**

Block Size: 11″ finished

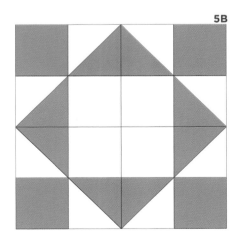

5B

6 arrange and sew

Lay out the blocks in rows. Each row is made up of 6 blocks and 6 rows are needed. Refer to the diagram on page 53 and notice how Block A and Block B alternate. After the blocks have been sewn into rows, press the seam allowances of the odd-numbered rows toward the right and the even-numbered rows toward the left to make the seams "nest."

Sew the rows together to complete the center of the quilt.

7 inner border

Cut (7) 2½″ strips across the width of the fabric. Sew the strips together end-to-end to make one long strip. Trim the borders from this strip.

Refer to Borders (pg. 102) in the Construction Basics to measure and cut the inner borders. The strips are approximately 66½″ for the sides and approximately 70½″ for the top and bottom.

8 outer border

Cut (8) 4″ strips across the width of the fabric. Sew the strips together end-to-end to make one long strip. Trim the borders from this strip.

Refer to Borders (pg. 102) in the Construction Basics to measure and cut the outer borders. The strips are approximately 70½″ for the sides and approximately 77½″ for the top and bottom.

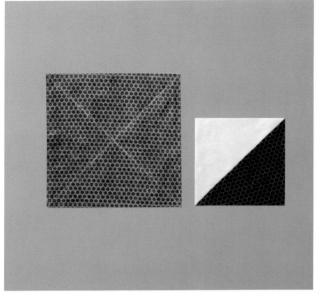

1 Make 4 half-square triangles by layering (2) 10″ squares together with right sides facing. Sew all the way around the outer edge using a ¼″ seam allowance. Cut from corner to corner twice on the diagonal. Open and press, then square each half-square triangle to 6½″. Stack all matching half-square triangles together.

2 Select 4 matching half-square triangles. Cut each in half vertically and horizontally.

3 Rearrange the pieces as shown. Make 4 quadrants and sew them together to make Block A. Make 18.

4 Select 4 matching half-square triangles and cut each in half vertically and horizontally as before. Rearrange the pieces as shown to make Block B. Make 18.

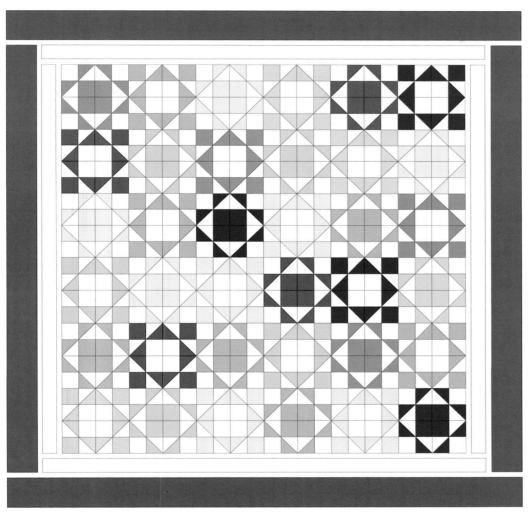

9 quilt and bind

Layer the quilt with batting and backing and quilt. After the quilting is complete, square up the quilt and trim away all excess batting and backing. Add binding to complete the quilt. See Construction Basics (pg. 102) for binding instructions.

For the tutorial and everything you need to make this quilt visit:
www.msqc.co/blockspring18

keyhole
quilt

I come from a family of pranksters. We are all such jokers and on any occasion we can find, there are bound to be plenty of hijinks afoot. For St. Patrick's Day we liked to keep things interesting by telling the kids that Leprechauns had dyed everything for breakfast green, from the pancakes to the eggs. We even squeezed a tiny drop of green food coloring into the kids' glasses, so when they poured in their milk, it instantly turned green! They always enjoyed that and soon began to come up with little jokes of their own.

In a family of seven children, you never knew when you might walk into your room to find your bed short-sheeted or every single item in sight turned upside down, including the picture frames on the wall. The kids pulled pranks on each other constantly—and still do—and they really come alive on April Fools' Day!

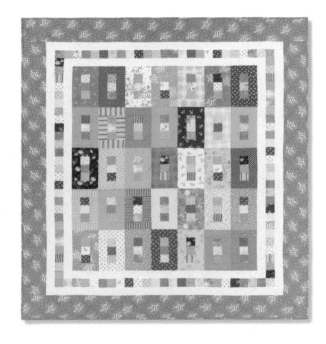

One year, my kids had set up the old "bucket of water on top of the door" trick. They were just coming into their own, prank-wise, and this was the biggest prank they'd pulled yet. The door creaked on its hinges under the weight of the bucket, sloshing water, and the kids squealed under their breaths in anticipation from their not-so-subtle hiding places, waiting for their unsuspecting dad to walk through the door.

As soon as poor Ron walked in, he was drenched from head to toe. The kids' prank had worked perfectly, just like in the movies. They rolled on the floor, laughing so hard they cried. Thankfully, my husband is a great sport and he laughed right along with them, but inside, he was plotting his revenge.

Later that day, after the hubbub had died down and Ron was in dry clothes once more, he made sure the kids were nowhere in sight and set up the bucket trick once more. He was determined to bait them with their own trap. The problem was, as he went about his chores for the rest of the day, he completely forgot about that bucket on top of the door and eventually walked right through it without a second thought!

For those who witnessed it, it was a complete and utter surprise, to him and to them! This time, the reaction was even more hilarious. It was an April Fools' Day that went down in history as the day Dad pranked himself.

materials

QUILT SIZE
65" x 73"

BLOCK SIZE
6" x 10" finished

QUILT TOP
1 roll of 2½" print strips

FIRST & THIRD BORDER
1 yard

OUTER BORDER
1¼ yards

BINDING
¾ yard

BACKING
4½ yards - vertical seam(s)

SAMPLE QUILT
Pepper and Flax by Corey Yoder
for Moda Fabrics

1 cut

From each of 35 print 2½" strips, cut:

- (4) 6½" rectangles. Stack all matching rectangles together. There will be a 14" – 16" piece left from each strip.

2 sew

Sew 3 of the remaining short strips together to make a strip set. Cut each strip set into 2½" x 6½" rectangles. Each strip set will yield 5 – 6 rectangles and a **total of 35** are needed for the blocks. The remaining pieces will be used for the

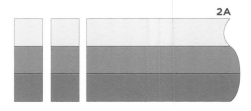

pieced border, so set them aside for that purpose.

 NOTE: *You have 2 short strips left over. Cut 1 of the longer pieces to the same length, and stitch the 3 together to make another strip set. Cut the remainder of the strip into 2½" squares and add to the pieces set aside for the borders.* **2A**

Sew 3 of the 4 remaining strips together into 1 strip set. Cut the strip set into 2½" x 6½" rectangles, for a **total of 16**. Add these to the pieces that were set aside for the pieced border.

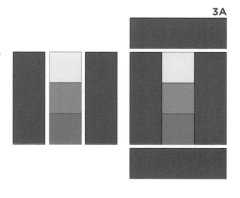

3A

3 block construction

Pick up a stack of 4 matching 2½" x 6½" rectangles. Sew a 2½" x 6½" rectangle to either side of a strip-pieced 2½" x 6½" rectangle. Add a 2½" x 6½" rectangle to the top and bottom to complete the block. **Make 35 blocks.** 3A

Block size: 6" x 10" finished

4 arrange and sew

Lay out the blocks in 5 rows of 7 across. When you're happy with the appearance, sew the rows together. Press the seam allowances in the odd rows toward the right and the even rows toward the left. This will make the seams "nest." Sew the rows together to complete the center of the quilt.

5 first border

Cut (5) 2½" strips across the width of the fabric. Sew the strips together end-to-end to make one long strip. Trim the borders from this strip.

Refer to Borders (pg. 102) in the Construction Basics to measure and cut the inner borders. The strips are approximately 50½" for the sides and approximately 46½" for the top and bottom.

6 pieced border

Measure the quilt top in several places vertically. The sides should measure approximately 54½". Pick up the strip-pieced rectangles that were set aside for the border. Sew 9 strip-pieced rectangles together to make a side border. **Make 2** and sew one to either side of the quilt. **Note:** If the pieced

border is a bit off, adjust the seam allowances over several places. Use a wider seam allowance if the border is too long or a smaller seam allowance if it is a bit too short. This will apply to the top and bottom borders as well.

Measure the quilt top in several places horizontally. The width of the quilt top should measure approximately 50½". Sew 8 strip-pieced rectangles together. Add (1) 2½" square to complete the strip. **Make 2** and sew one to the top and one to the bottom of the quilt.

7 third border

Cut (6) 2½" strips across the width of the fabric. Sew the strips together end-to-end to make one long strip. Trim the borders from this strip.

Refer to Borders (pg. 102) in the Construction Basics to measure and cut the third borders. The strips are approximately 58½" for the sides and approximately 54½" for the top and bottom.

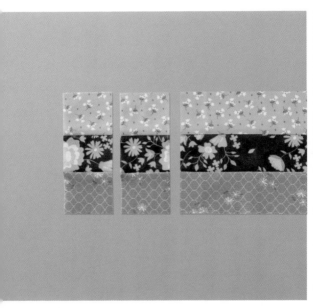

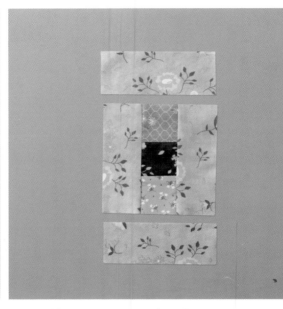

1   Sew (3) 2½″ strips together along the length.
    Cut each strip set into 2½″ x 6½″ rectangles.

2   Sew a 2½″ x 6½″ rectangle to either side of a strip-pieced
    rectangle.

3   Add a 2½″ x 6½″ rectangle to the top
    and bottom to complete the block.

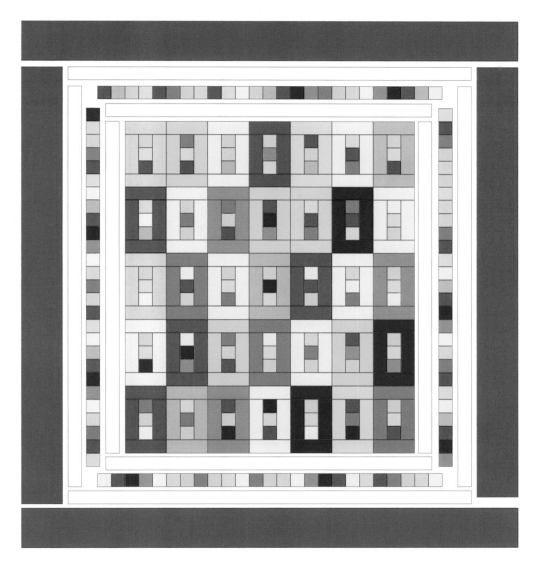

8 outer border

Cut (7) 6″ strips across the width of the fabric. Sew the strips together end-to-end to make one long strip. Trim the borders from this strip.

Refer to Borders (pg. 102) in the Construction Basics to measure and cut the outer borders. The strips are approximately 62½″ for the sides and approximately 65½″ for the top and bottom.

9 quilt and bind

Layer the quilt with batting and backing and quilt. After the quilting is complete, square up the quilt and trim away all excess batting and backing. Add binding to complete the quilt. See Construction Basics (pg. 102) for binding instructions.

For the tutorial and everything
you need to make this quilt visit:
www.msqc.co/blockspring18

62

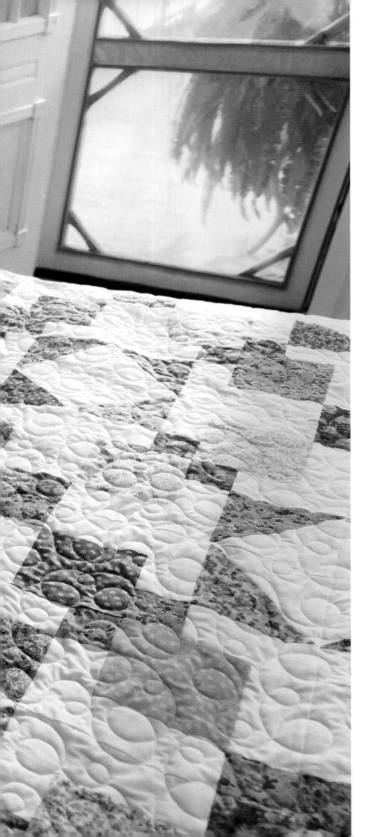

nine-patch **madness**

The best Mother's Day gifts come straight from the heart. When I was a girl, I always gave my mother a hand-drawn card and a corsage made from flowers I picked in the backyard garden. Year after year, my mother made a fuss over my homemade gifts. All day long she wore the flowers with pride. She made me feel like my corsages were the most beautiful she had ever seen.

When it comes to gifts, it's the thought that counts. When a mother receives a macaroni necklace strung with all the love a chubby-cheeked kindergartner has to offer, you can bet it will be treasured as if it were twenty-four karat gold.

I'll never forget the year my friend, Pam, was treated to a Mother's Day breakfast in bed by her three young children. That year her husband happened to be away on business, and she wasn't expecting any special treatment. So when she was awakened by a chorus of hushed giggles coming from the other side of the bedroom door, she was completely taken by surprise.

"Mama! Are you awake? We have a surprise for you." In burst her three children, still in their pajamas. "We made breakfast!"

Now, Pam did not live the kind of life in which breakfast in bed was a common occurrence and she did not own a bed tray. Instead, her special breakfast was precariously balanced on an old cookie sheet.

"I cooked the eggs myself, Mom." Her oldest child, eight-year-old Micah, beamed with pride. "I did the toast too. I even scraped off where it got burned." Pam surveyed the gigantic serving of runny scrambled eggs and burnt toast.

"I made you a special drink!" five-year-old Thomas exclaimed. "I just mixed up orange juice and milk. It's

a new invention: Creamy orange juice! You're gonna love it, Mom!"

"And I got these flowers just for you, Mama!" Three-year-old Kimberly held out a bouquet of dandelion blooms. Pam held the flowers up to her nose and smiled.

"They are lovely. Thank you, Sweetheart."

The kids climbed up on the bed and watched with wide eyes as Pam ate. With each runny bite—and each labored sip—Pam made sure to react with kindness and gratitude. How could she not? That meal had been prepared with so much love and enthusiasm, she couldn't help but feel adored. Of course, the next year she made sure to request a simple breakfast of cereal and milk—hold the creamy orange juice.

materials

QUILT SIZE
81" X 94"

BLOCK SIZE
13" finished

QUILT TOP
4 packages 5" print squares
4 packages 5" background squares

INNER BORDER
1 yard

OUTER BORDER
1¾ yards

BINDING
¾ yard

BACKING
7½ yards - horizontal seam(s)
  or 3 yards - 108" wide

SAMPLE QUILT
Amorette by Kaye England for
Wilmington Fabrics

1 make 9-patches

Lay out (9) 5" squares in 3 rows of
3 alternating print and background
squares. Sew each row together. Press
the seam allowances of the first and
third rows toward the left and the center
row toward the right to make the seams
"nest." Sew all 3 rows together. **1A**

2 cut

Align a ruler with the seam between the
first and second squares. Measure out
2¼" from the sewn seam. Cut the block
in half vertically. Without moving any of
the pieces, measure 2¼" from the sewn
seam between the first and second
squares and cut in half horizontally. **2A**

1A

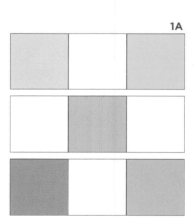

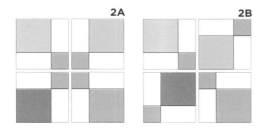

Turn the upper right and lower left corners of the block 90 degrees. The small squares will be positioned on the outer edge of the block. **2B**

3 sew

Sew the block back together. **3A**

From the background fabric being used for the inner border, cut (2) 5″ strips across the width of the fabric. Subcut the strips into 5″ squares. Each strip will yield 8 squares and you need an additional 12 squares. Add them to the 4 packages of 5″ background squares.

Set aside the remaining background fabric for the inner border.

Pick up (2) 5″ background squares and draw a line from corner to corner on the reverse side of the squares. Draw another line ½″ from the first. Place the square atop the upper left and lower right quadrant of the block. Sew on the longest drawn line. Move the block so the shortest drawn line is placed under your needle and sew on the line. Cut at the halfway point between the 2 sewn seams. Set aside the small half-square

triangle units you have trimmed off for our bonus project. **3B**

Make 30 blocks.

Block size: 13″ finished

4 arrange and sew

Lay out the blocks in 6 rows with each row made up of 5 blocks. Refer to the diagram on page 69 to see how the blocks are arranged. Sew the blocks together. Press the seam allowances of the odd rows toward the right and the even rows toward the left to make the seams "nest." Sew the rows together.

5 inner border

Cut (8) 2½″ strips across the width of the fabric. Sew the strips together end-to-end to make one long strip. Trim the borders from this strip.

Refer to Borders (pg. 102) in the Construction Basics to measure and cut the inner borders. The strips are approximately 78½″ for the sides and approximately 69½″ for the top and bottom.

6 outer border

Cut (9) 6½″ strips across the width of the fabric. Sew the strips together end-to-end to make one long strip. Trim the borders from this strip.

Refer to Borders (pg. 102) in the Construction Basics to measure and

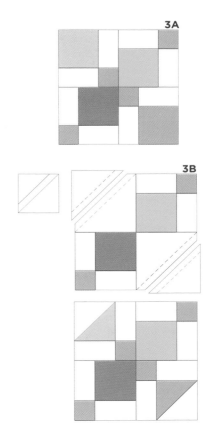

cut the outer borders. The strips are approximately 82½″ for the sides and approximately 81½″ for the top and bottom.

7 quilt and bind

Layer the quilt with batting and backing and quilt. After the quilting is complete, square up the quilt and trim away all excess batting and backing. Add binding to complete the quilt. See Construction Basics (pg. 102) for binding instructions.

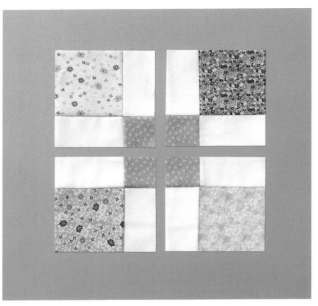

1 Lay out (9) 5″ squares in 3 rows of 3 alternating print and background squares as shown. Sew the rows together to make a 9-patch block.

2 Cut the 9-patch block in half vertically and horizontally.

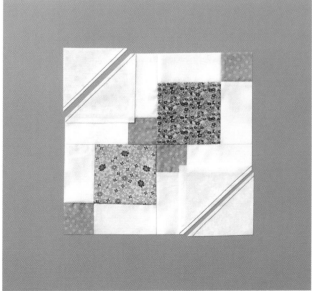

3 Turn the upper right and lower left quadrants of the block 90°.

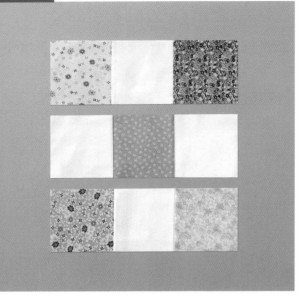

4 Sew the 4 quadrants back together.

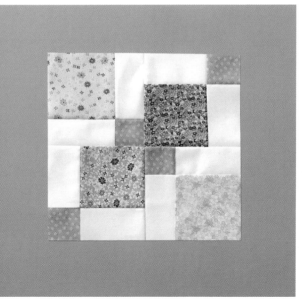

5 Draw a line from corner to corner once on the diagonal of (2) 5″ background squares. Draw another line ½″ from the first. Place one square on the upper left corner and the other on the lower right. Sew on both marked lines. Cut between the sewn seams. Set aside the extra half-square triangles for the bonus project.

6 Press the seam allowances on the corner half-square triangles toward the darker fabric.

BONUS PROJECT:
FLYING GEESE TABLE RUNNER

materials

TABLE RUNNER SIZE
20" x 55¾"

BLOCK SIZE
3¼" x 6½" finished

TABLE RUNNER
60 bonus half-square triangles

INNER BORDER
¼ yard

OUTER BORDER
½ yards

BINDING
½ yard

BACKING
1¾ yards - vertical seam(s)

SAMPLE QUILT
Amorette by Kaye England for Wilmington Fabrics

1 square up blocks

Square up all bonus half-square triangle units to 3¾".

2 sew

Sew the half-square triangle units into flying geese units. **Make 16** units with the print half-square triangles touching in the center. We'll call these flying geese A. **2A**

Make the remaining flying geese units with the white half-square triangle units touching in the center. We'll call these flying geese B. **2B**

Block Size: 3¼" x 6½" finished

2A **2B**

3 arrange and sew

Lay out the flying geese units into 2 rows. Alternate the flying geese A units with the flying geese B units. Each row is made up of 15 flying geese. Refer to the layout on the right, if necessary.

4 inner border

Cut (4) 1½" strips across the width of the fabric. Sew the strips together end-to-end to make one long strip. Trim the borders from this strip.

Refer to Borders (pg. 102) in the Construction Basics to measure and cut the inner borders. The strips are approximately 13½" for the sides and approximately 51¼" for the top and bottom.

5 outer border

Cut (4) 3" strips across the width of the fabric. Sew the strips together end-to-end to make one long strip. Trim the borders from this strip.

Refer to Borders (pg. 102) in the Construction Basics to measure and cut the outer borders. The strips are approximately 15½" for the sides and approximately 56¼" for the top and bottom.

6 quilt and bind

Layer the quilt with batting and backing and quilt. After the quilting is complete, square up the quilt and trim away all excess batting and backing. Add binding to complete the quilt. See Construction Basics (pg. 102) for binding instructions.

For the tutorial and everything
you need to make this quilt visit:
www.msqc.co/blockspring18

one
direction

Mothers everywhere let out a collective sigh when they hear their daughters singing along to their favorite boy bands at the top of their lungs behind closed bedroom doors. From the early days with those mop-topped Beatles singing out boldly, "I want to hold your hand" to modern chart toppers like One Direction telling shy girls everywhere they're beautiful, there's just something about well-dressed boys with sweet voices that make our cheeks blush.

Joy was definitely no exception. At the tender age of thirteen, she was enthralled with the New Kids on the Block. She could tell you all their names: Joey, Jordan, Jonathan, Danny, and Donnie—who happened to be her favorite, with his long, blonde ponytail that went all the way down his back.

It wasn't long before she heard that the New Kids on the Block were coming to her hometown for a concert. It was a wildly anticipated event for her friends at school. Most already had tickets and announced proudly that they

were going, but not Joy. She listened with feigned excitement as they described their seats and what they were going to wear, nodding along, but feeling as empty inside as a deflated balloon.

On the night of the concert, Joy languished in her room after refusing dinner, wishing that she were headed to the concert with her friends. She sat dejectedly, painting her toenails and listening to a well-worn cassette tape that featured such hits as "The Right Stuff" and "I'll Be Loving You," when she heard her phone ring. It was her friend Shawna.

Joy nearly dropped the phone when she realized Shawna was inviting her along to the concert! Becky had gotten sick and couldn't go at the last minute. Although Joy was concerned for her friend, this was the best news she'd ever gotten in her life. Finally, she would get to see her beloved Donnie in person!

At the enormous coliseum, the line out the door snaked into the parking lot where the girls stood in line, clutching their tickets in feverish hands. The concert was a dream come true and the girls screamed their hearts out, singing at the top of their lungs with every word. And Joy made sure to bring dear Becky an autographed T-shirt to school when she felt better.

Years later, when the New Kids on the Block went on tour again, they all attended the concert together. This time, thankfully, nobody got sick. And Donnie was cuter than ever!

materials

QUILT SIZE
82" x 91½" finished

BLOCK SIZE
8½" x 14" finished and 3½" x 7" finished

QUILT TOP
1 package 10" print squares
5½ yards background fabric – includes inner border and bonus projects

INNER BORDER
¾ yards

OUTER BORDER
1¾ yards

BINDING
¾ yard

BACKING
6 yards – vertical seam(s)

OTHER
Poly-Fil for bonus pillow projects

SAMPLE QUILT
Bloom Where You're Planted by Lori Whitlock for Riley Blake Designs

1 cut

Cut each of (39) 10" squares in half to make (2) 5" x 10" rectangles. Trim 1 of the rectangles to 5" x 9". Stack all matching pieces together. Cut (2) 5" squares from 1 of the remaining 10" print squares and set them aside for the bonus projects. Set the 2 remaining 10" squares aside for another project.

From the background fabric, cut:
*   (10) 5" strips across the width of the fabric – subcut each strip into 5" squares. Each strip will yield 8 squares and a **total of 78** are needed. Set the remaining 2 squares aside for the bonus project.

*   (20) 2½" strips across the width of the fabric – subcut each strip into 2½" x 10" rectangles. Each strip will yield 4 rectangles and a **total of 78** are needed. Set the remainder of the background fabric aside for sashing strips, inner border and bonus projects.

2 sew

Pick up a matching set of rectangles. Sew a 2½" x 10" background rectangle to each side of a 5" x 10" rectangle. **2A**

Draw a line from corner to corner once on the diagonal on the reverse side of (2) 5" background squares. Draw another line on each square ½" away from the first. **2B**

Place a marked background square on one end of the 5" x 9" rectangle with right sides facing. Sew on the longest marked line. Move the block so the shortest drawn line is placed under the needle of your sewing machine and sew on the line. Cut at the halfway point between the 2 sewn seams. Repeat for the other end of the rectangle. Set aside the small half-square triangles, keeping all matching units together. We'll be using those later. 2C

Sew the 2 sections together to complete 1 arrow block. **Make 39.** Set aside 3 arrows for the bonus projects. 2D

Pick up 21 pairs of matching small half-square triangles. Square each to 4". Sew a pair together to make a flying geese block. Repeat for the remaining 20 pairs. 2E

3 lay out and sew

Sew 9 arrow blocks together into a vertical row. **Make 4 rows.** Sew 2 rows together. Repeat for the remaining 2 rows. Set aside for the moment. 3A

Cut (4) 2½" strips across the width of the background fabric you set aside earlier to make sashing strips. Measure the rows of sewn arrow blocks (approximately 77"). Sew 2 strips together and trim each to your measurement. Sew a strip to the pointed edge of the arrow strips. 3B

Sew 21 flying geese together into a vertical row. Cut a 3½" x 7½" rectangle from the background fabric and stitch it to the bottom of the row. 3C

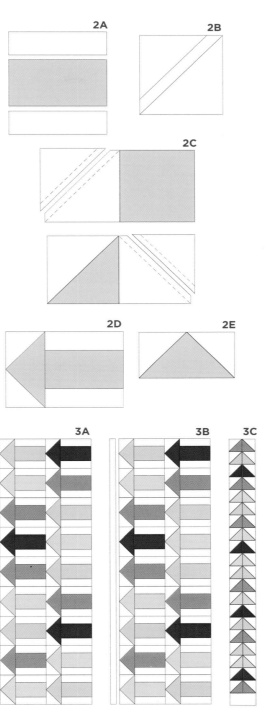

Sew the 3 sections together. Trim the center section to match the arrow sections on either side. See the diagram to the bottom left.

4 inner border

Cut (8) 2½" strips across the width of the fabric. Sew the strips together end-to-end to make one long strip. Trim the borders from this strip.

Refer to Borders (pg. 102) in the Construction Basics to measure and cut the inner borders. The strips are approximately 77" for the sides and approximately 71½" for the top and bottom.

5 outer border

Cut (9) 6" strips across the width of the fabric. Sew the strips together end-to-end to make one long strip. Trim the borders from this strip.

Refer to Borders (pg. 102) in the Construction Basics to measure and cut the outer borders. The strips are approximately 81" for the sides and approximately 82½" for the top and bottom.

6 quilt and bind

Layer the quilt with batting and backing and quilt. After the quilting is complete, square up the quilt and trim away all excess batting and backing. Add binding to complete the quilt. See Construction Basics (pg. 102) for binding instructions.

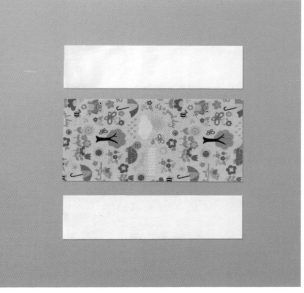

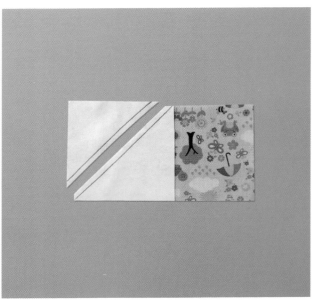

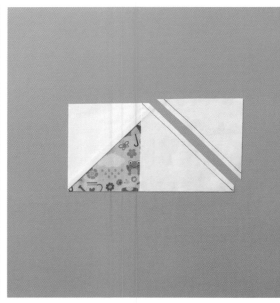

1 Sew a 2½" x 10" background rectangle to each side of a 5" x 10" rectangle.

2 Place a marked background square on one end of the 5" x 9" rectangle with right sides facing. Sew on both marked lines. Cut at the halfway point between the sewn seams.

3 Place another marked background square on the other end of the 5" x 9" rectangle with right sides facing. Sew on both marked lines and cut at the halfway point between the sewn seams.

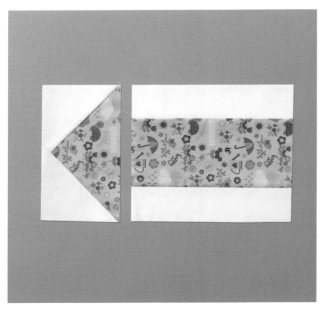

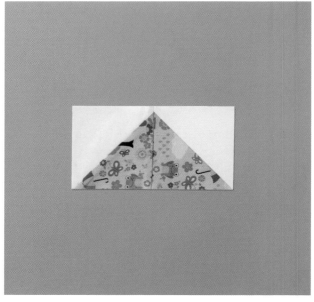

4 Sew the 2 sections together to complete 1 arrow block.

5 Make flying geese units by sewing 2 matching half-square triangles together.

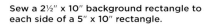

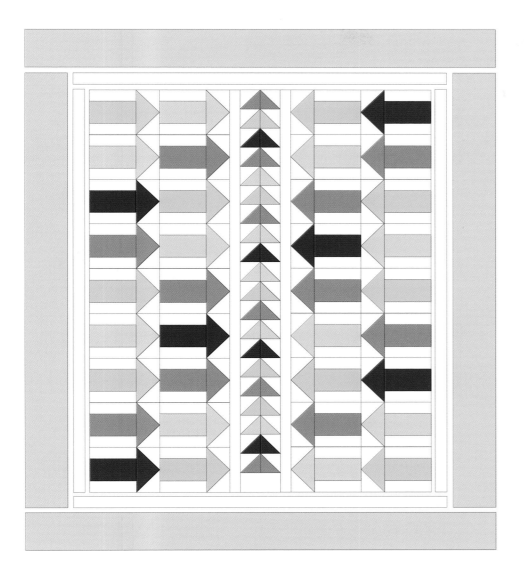

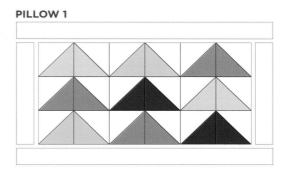

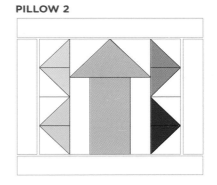

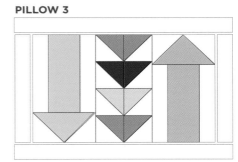

BONUS PROJECT:
ONE DIRECTION PILLOWS

Pick up the (2) 5″ background squares you set aside earlier. Draw a line from corner to corner once on the diagonal on the reverse side of each square. Layer a marked background square with a 5″ print square that was also set aside earlier, with right sides facing. Sew on both sides of the line using a ¼″ seam allowance. Open to reveal 2 half-square triangle units. Repeat for the remaining background and print square. Square each unit to 4″. Keep the matching prints together and add them to the stack of small half-square triangles. **1A**

 NOTE: *If you choose to quilt the pillow tops, you'll need to add a piece of batting and backing to the pillow front and do the quilting before adding the pillow back. Left over scraps you have on hand will work nicely.*

Pillow 1

Pillow Size: 25″ x 18″ finished

1 cut

From the background fabric, cut:

- (2) 2½″ strips across the width of the fabric
- (1) 25½″ x 18½″ rectangle

2 sew

Pick up 12 pairs of small matching half-square triangles. Square each half-square triangle to 4″. Sew 2 matching half-square triangles together to make 1 flying geese unit. **Make 12. 2A**

Sew 4 flying geese units together to make a vertical row. **Make 3 rows** and sew them together. **2B**

Sew the (2) 2½″ background strips together end-to-end. Cut the borders from this strip. Measure the pillow horizontally and vertically. The top and bottom borders are sewn on first and each should measure approximately 21½″. The side borders are sewn on last. Each should measure approximately 18½″.

Layer the 25½″ x 18½″ rectangle with the front of the pillow with right sides facing. Sew around the perimeter using a ¼″ to ½″ seam allowance and leaving a gap large enough to use when filling the pillow (about 3″ – 5″). Take a few backstitches at the beginning and the end of the seam.

 NOTE: *If you use a larger seam allowance, your pillow may be a little smaller than the given size.*

Turn the pillow right side out and stuff with Poly-Fil. Whipstitch the opening in the seam allowance closed.

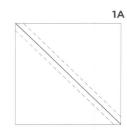

1A

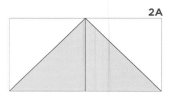

2A

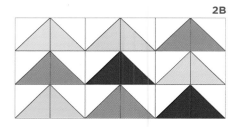

2B

Pillow 2

Pillow Size: 19½″ x 18″

1 cut

From the background fabric, cut:

- (2) 2½″ strips across the width of the fabric
- (1) 20″ x 18½″ rectangle

2 sew

Pick up 4 matching sets of small half-square triangles. Square each half-square triangle unit to 4″. Sew each set together as shown to make a flying geese. **Make 4. 2A**

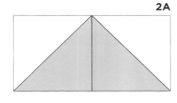

2A

2B

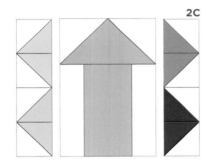

2C

Sew 2 flying geese together as shown to make 1 strip. **Make 2.** 2B

Sew a flying geese strip to either side of an arrow block. 2C

Sew the (2) 2½" strips of background fabric together end-to-end. From the strip, cut 2 pieces that measure 2½" x 16" and sew one to the top of the pillow and one to the bottom. Cut 2 pieces that measure 2½" x 18½". Sew one to either side of the pillow to complete the top.

Layer the 20" x 18½" rectangle with the front of the pillow with right sides facing. Sew around the perimeter using a ¼" to ½" seam allowance and leaving a gap large enough to use when filling the pillow (about 3" – 5"). Take a few backstitches at the beginning and the end of the seam.

 NOTE: *If you use a larger seam allowance, your pillow may be a little smaller than the given size.*

Turn the pillow right side out and stuff with Poly-Fil. Whipstitch the opening in the seam allowance closed.

Pillow 3

Pillow Size: 28" x 18"

1 cut

From the background fabric, cut:

- (2) 2½" strips across the width of the fabric
- (1) 28½" x 18½" rectangle

2 sew

Pick up 4 sets of matching small half-square triangles. Square each half-square triangle unit to 4". Sew a pair together to make a flying geese. **Make 4**. Sew the 4 geese into a vertical row as shown. 2A

Sew an arrow block to either side of the vertical row of flying geese. Notice that the arrows are pointing in opposite directions. 2B

Sew the (2) 2½" strips of background fabric together end-to-end. Cut the borders from the strip. Cut 2 strips 24½" long and sew one to the top and one to the bottom of the pillow top.

Cut 2 strips 18½" long and sew one to either side of the top.

Layer the 28½" x 18½" rectangle with the front of the pillow with right sides facing. Sew around the perimeter using a ¼" to ½" seam allowance and leaving a gap large enough to use when filling the pillow (about 3" – 5"). Take a few backstitches at the beginning and the end of the seam.

 NOTE: *If you use a larger seam allowance, your pillow may be a little smaller than the given size.*

Turn the pillow right side out and stuff with Poly-Fil. Whipstitch the opening in the seam allowance closed.

2A

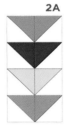

2B

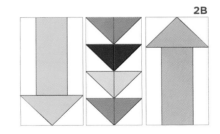

For the tutorial and everything you need to make this quilt visit:
www.msqc.co/blockspring18

slanted half-hex

There is a flower child in me who adores everything about the earth and wants peace, love, and harmony more than anything. I want to wear daisies in my hair and dance in a meadow. And maybe I will one of these days. But even more importantly, I want to take good care of the earth. I feel a responsibility to do what's right and reduce, reuse, and recycle. All of those things matter to me. I want to leave this world better than I found it in whatever way I can.

Earth Day is just around the corner and I remember those days when we would plant a tree or clean up garbage to honor our wonderful world. But what can we do as quilters? Well, the answer is easier than you might think—make a quilt! Even better, make a quilt and donate it to someone in need.

Quilters are some of the greenest people I know. Every time I teach a class, there is always someone who says, "If you are throwing away your scraps, here is a basket for them." At a recent quilt show, I saw a quilt that was made entirely out of tiny pieces of fabric that other people were throwing out! It was amazing.

I am so proud of quilters! We make do and reuse scraps of fabric that would be overlooked by almost everyone else. We take old clothing and recycle it into gorgeous memory quilts. Way back in the day, quilters would even take the pretty calico fabrics from feed sacks and make quilts and clothing with those fabrics. It's been our way of life from the beginning. Quilters scrimp and save and use every last scrap. We can't bear to let go of fabric that could be used for something else. And if that isn't green, I don't know what is!

If you need a few ideas for your fabric scraps, here are some to get you started:

* Keep all your scraps and use them for stuffing in a pet bed
* Create a cute zipper pouch
* Sew long strips together into one long piece and crochet them into rugs or just about anything you can think of

* Make a set of pieced pillow covers and fill the pillows with the leftover scraps
* Stitch together a set of scrappy coasters
* Make a wallet and a matching keychain fob
* Create a gorgeous piece of art
* Cover buttons
* Make hair bows
* Piece a scrappy binding for your quilt
* Make doll clothes
* Use small pieces to appliqué onto quilt blocks
* And so much more!

If you have any great ideas for scrap busting projects, we'd love to see them. Be sure to share them with us this Earth Day using the hashtag **#makesomethingtoday.** Keep on doing what you do, quilters, and together we can make this world a more beautiful place!

materials

QUILT SIZE
76¾" x 77"

BLOCK SIZE
4" x 9½" finished

QUILT TOP
1 package 10" print squares
1 package 10" background squares

INNER BORDER
¾ yard

OUTER BORDER
1½ yard

BINDING
¾ yard

BACKING
5 yards 44" wide fabric – vertical seam(s)

OTHER
Large MSQC Half-Hexagon Template for 10" Squares

SAMPLE QUILT
Blush by My Mind's Eye for Riley Blake Fabrics

1 cut

Layer 2 or 3 print squares together and fold in half with right sides facing. Align the top of the Half-Hexagon template with the raw edges of the squares and the sides of the template with the sides of the squares and cut out the shapes. Each 10" square will yield 2 half-hexagons and a **total of 72** are needed for the quilt.

Repeat for the background squares, cutting out a **total of 72** half-hexagons.

2 lay out blocks

Lay out the half-hexagons in rows. Each row is made up of 8 half-hexagons and the print rows alternate with the background rows. Do not sew anything together until all the rows are laid out and you are happy with the appearance.

Row 1 (top row) is made up of print half-hexagons. Notice the piece has the longest edge facing the bottom of the quilt. Row 2 is made up of background half-hexagons and the longest edge touches the edge of the print above it. **2A**

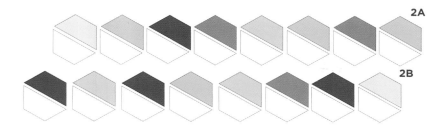

2A

2B

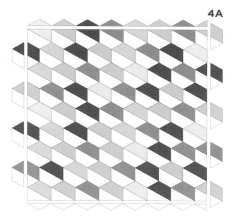

4A

Row 3 is made just like Row 1 but is offset so the pieces will fit together. Row 4 is made just like row 2 and is offset so the pieces will match up with the prints in row 3. **2B**

Continue laying out the print rows and the background rows until you have a **total of 18** rows laid out. **2C**

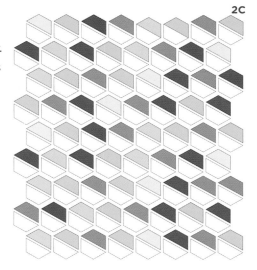

2C

3 sew

Instead of sewing the rows together horizontally as usual, we are going to switch tactics and sew the half-hexagons together by stitching the pieces together in diagonal rows. When you are done sewing each diagonal row, replace it on the design wall until each row has been sewn together. Refer to the diagram on the right. **3A**

Now that all the diagonal rows have been made, sew the rows together. Just a hint, it's easiest to sew the corner pieces on last.

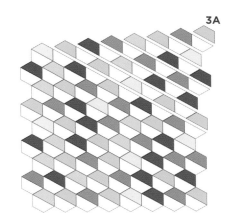

3A

4 trim

Align a ruler with the even edges of the offset rows along the side of the quilt top. Trim to make the edges even. Repeat for the other side of the quilt.

Trim the top and bottom of the quilt top by aligning the ruler with the bottom edge of each peak. Be careful not to trim off the seam allowances. **4A**

5 inner border

Cut (7) 2½″ strips across the width of the fabric. Sew the strips together end-to-end to make one long strip. Trim the borders from this strip.

Refer to Borders (pg. 102) in the Construction Basics to measure and cut the inner borders. The strips are approximately 62½″ for the sides and approximately 66¼″ for the top and bottom.

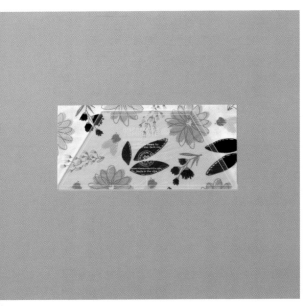

1 Using the Missouri Star Quilt Co. Half-Hexagon template, fold a 10″ square in half and cut 2 pieces.

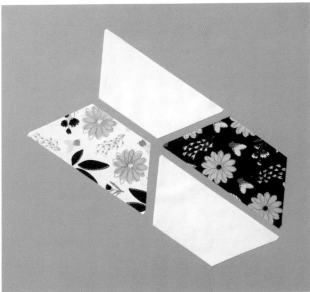

2 Lay out the half-hexagons in rows. Each row is made up of 8 half-hexagons and the print rows alternate with background rows. Do not sew anything together until all the rows are laid out.

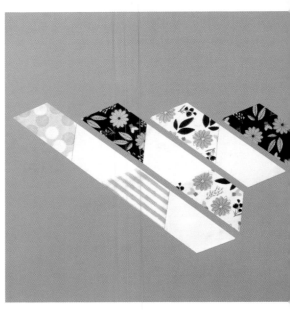

3 After the rows are laid out and you're happy with the appearance, sew the pieces together into diagonal rows.

6 outer border

Cut (8) 6″ strips across the width of the fabric. Sew the strips together end-to-end to make one long strip. Trim the borders from this strip.

Refer to Borders (pg. 102) in the Construction Basics to measure and cut the outer borders. The strips are approximately 66½″ for the sides and approximately 77¼″ for the top and bottom.

7 quilt and bind

Layer the quilt with batting and backing and quilt. After the quilting is complete, square up the quilt and trim away all excess batting and backing. Add binding to complete the quilt. See Construction Basics (pg. 102) for binding instructions.

put a pin in it

Pincushions are as essential to sewing as a palette is for painting. They might be simple or extravagant, but without them, things can get complicated. We all know what happens when pins get left around. I'm sorry to say that I've lost my fair share of needles in the rug or the couch and that's no picnic. Especially for my poor husband!

Well, there's no need to (literally) sit on pins and needles anymore! Pick up your favorite pincushion and give it the praise it deserves. Or go ahead and make yourself a new one. After all, it's probably been years since you got that cute, little tomato and it's definitely seen better days.

A pincushion is a fast, fun project that makes a great gift for a friend as well as a pretty accent for your sewing room. No matter how many you have, you can always use one more. And with the incredible variety we see in the quilting world, there's bound to be one that fits your personal style and works wonderfully for your needs.

On my sewing table, I have three of my favorites. One is the traditional tomato and strawberry, another is shaped like a chicken, and the last is bright pink and magnetic. Each is useful and interesting.

When I travel, I'm always fascinated with all the clever pincushions I see. I like to think they give me a glimpse into the personality of the quilters I meet.

Have you ever tried to make your own pincushion? If you haven't, you're in for a treat! Practically anything can become a pincushion; old salt cellars, planters, candle holders, teacups with saucers, antique zinc canning lids, and so on. No matter what you choose as a container, you can count on it being adorable!

1. Select the base or container you would like to use for your pincushion.

2. Measure the opening of the container. You don't need to be too precise, just make sure you have a piece of fabric approximately twice as large as the opening.

3. Cut a circular shape from the fabric and sew a running stitch all the way around about ¼" from the edge.

4. Gather the circular shape into a loose pouch by pulling on the running stitch and leaving the needle and tail of the thread hanging.

5. Fill the pouch with Poly-Fil stuffing beads, excess batting, shredded fabric scraps, or ground walnut shells (available in any pet store and sold as lizard litter).

6. Stitch the pouch securely closed and glue it into your chosen container with a strong adhesive. We recommend E6000 glue.

7. After the glue has dried, add your favorite pins. You're all ready to sew!

When you're all through, take a moment to admire your handiwork, and then make a few more! They're so easy to put together and make beautiful gifts. I hope you have fun with this project, the possibilities are truly endless.

4 x 4
quilt

QUILT SIZE
70" x 78" finished

BLOCK SIZE
8" finished

QUILT TOP
1 roll of 2½" print strips
1¾ yards background – includes
inner border

OUTER BORDER
1¼ yards

BINDING
¾ yard

BACKING
5 yards - vertical seam(s)

SAMPLE QUILT
Longitude Batiks by Kate Spain
for Moda Fabrics

QUILTING PATTERN
Free Swirls

ONLINE TUTORIALS
msqc.co/blockspring18

PATTERN
pg. 6

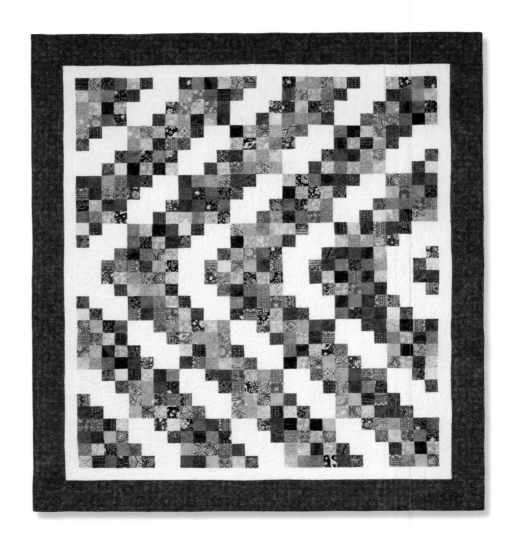

bordered
nine-patch

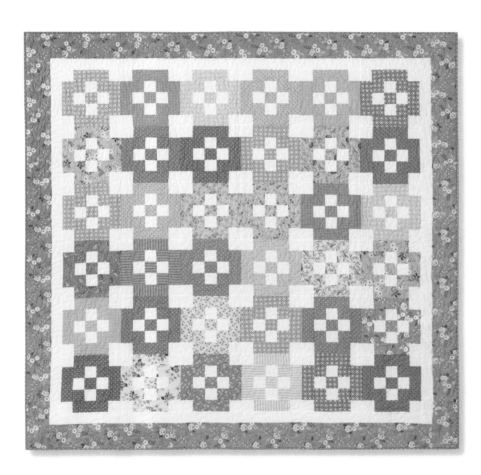

QUILT SIZE
73" x 73"

BLOCK SIZE
10" finished

QUILT TOP
1 roll of 2½" print strips
1¾ yards background fabric – includes
inner border

OUTER BORDER
1¼ yards

BINDING
¾ yard

BACKING
4½ yards - vertical seam(s)

SAMPLE QUILT
Nest by Lella Boutique for Moda Fabrics

QUILTING PATTERN
Birds

ONLINE TUTORIALS
msqc.co/blockspring18

PATTERN
pg. 14

card
trick

QUILT SIZE
82½" x 93¾"

BLOCK SIZE
11¼" finished

QUILT TOP
1 roll of 2½" print strips
4¾ yards background
fabric –
   includes inner border

OUTER BORDER
1¾ yards

BINDING
¾ yard

BACKING
8½ yards - vertical
seam(s)
or 2¾ yards - 108" wide

SAMPLE QUILT
Monday, Monday by Jill
Finley of Penny Rose
Fabrics for Riley Blake
Designs

QUILTING PATTERN
Loops and Swirls

ONLINE TUTORIALS
msqc.co/blockspring18

PATTERN
pg. 22

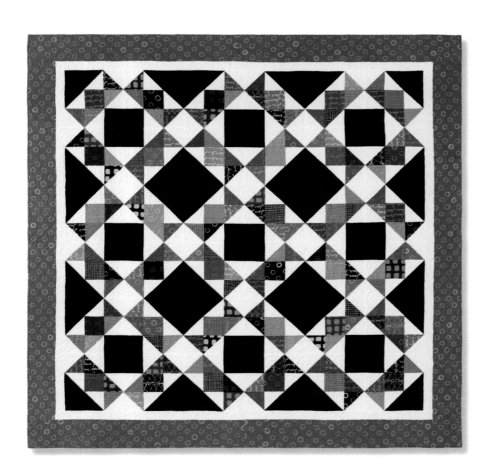

crown
quilt

QUILT SIZE
88" X 88" finished

BLOCK SIZE
24" finished

QUILT TOP
3 packages 5" print squares
3 packages 5" white squares
2 yards contrasting fabric
   (we used black)

INNER BORDER
¾ yards

OUTER BORDER
1¾ yards

BINDING
¾ yard

BACKING
8 yards - vertical seam(s) or
2¾ yards - 108" wide.

SAMPLE QUILT
Mark to Make by Malka Dubrawsky
for Robert Kaufman

QUILTING PATTERN
Variety

ONLINE TUTORIALS
msqc.co/blockspring18

PATTERN
pg. 30

disappearing pinwheel basket

QUILT SIZE
78" x 78"

BLOCK SIZE
11" finished

QUILT TOP
1 package 10" print squares
1 package of 10" background
squares

OUTER BORDER
1½ yards

BINDING
¾ yard

BACKING
7¼ yards - vertical seam(s)
or 2½ yards - 108" wide

SAMPLE QUILT
Roaring Twenties by Snow Leopard
Designs for Free Spirit Fabrics

QUILTING PATTERN
Posies

ONLINE TUTORIALS
msqc.co/blockspring18

PATTERN
pg. 38

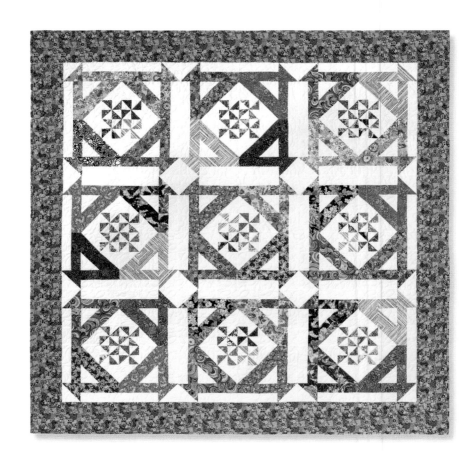

half & half

QUILT SIZE
77" X 77"

BLOCK SIZE
11" finished

QUILT TOP
1 package 10" print squares
1 package 10" background squares

INNER BORDER
¾ yard

OUTER BORDER
1 yard

BINDING
¾ yard

BACKING
4¾ yards - vertical seam(s)

SAMPLE QUILT
Sequoia by Edyta Sitar of Laundry Basket Quilts for Andover Fabrics

QUILTING PATTERN
Birds

ONLINE TUTORIALS
msqc.co/blockspring18

PATTERN
pg. 46

keyhole

QUILT SIZE
65" x 73"

BLOCK SIZE
6" x 10" finished

QUILT TOP
1 roll of 2½" print strips

FIRST & THIRD BORDER
1 yard

OUTER BORDER
1¼ yards

BINDING
¾ yard

BACKING
4½ yards - vertical seam(s)

SAMPLE QUILT
Pepper and Flax by Corey Yoder
for Moda Fabrics

QUILTING PATTERN
Sticky Buns

ONLINE TUTORIALS
msqc.co/blockspring18

PATTERN
pg. 54

nine-patch madness

QUILT SIZE
81" X 94"

BLOCK SIZE
13" finished

QUILT TOP
4 packages 5" print squares
4 packages 5" background squares

INNER BORDER
1 yard

OUTER BORDER
1¾ yards

BINDING
¾ yard

BACKING
7½ yards - horizontal seam(s)
    or 3 yards - 108" wide

SAMPLE QUILT
Amorette by Kaye England for
Wilmington Fabrics

QUILTING PATTERN
Loops and Swirls

ONLINE TUTORIALS
msqc.co/blockspring18

PATTERN
pg. 62

one direction

QUILT SIZE
82" x 91½" finished

BLOCK SIZE
8½" x 14" finished and 3½" x 7"
  finished

QUILT TOP
1 package 10" print squares
5½ yards background fabric –
  includes inner border and bonus
  projects

INNER BORDER
¾ yards

OUTER BORDER
1¾ yards

BINDING
¾ yard

BACKING
6 yards – vertical seam(s)

OTHER
Poly-Fil for bonus pillow projects

SAMPLE QUILT
Bloom Where You're Planted by Lori
Whitlock for Riley Blake Designs

QUILTING PATTERN
Free Swirls

ONLINE TUTORIALS
msqc.co/blockspring18

PATTERN
pg. 72

slanted half-hex

QUILT SIZE
76¾" x 77"

BLOCK SIZE
4" x 9½" finished

QUILT TOP
1 package 10" print squares
1 package 10" background
  squares

INNER BORDER
¾ yard

OUTER BORDER
1½ yard

BINDING
¾ yard

BACKING
5 yards 44" wide fabric –
  vertical seam(s)

OTHER
Large MSQC Half-Hexagon
  Template for 10" Squares

SAMPLE QUILT
Blush by My Mind's Eye for Riley
Blake Fabrics

QUILTING PATTERN
Paisley Feathers

ONLINE TUTORIALS
msqc.co/blockspring18

PATTERN
pg. 82

construction basics

general quilting

- All seams are ¼" inch unless directions specify differently.
- Cutting instructions are given at the point when cutting is required.
- Precuts are not prewashed; therefore do not prewash other fabrics in the project.
- All strips are cut width of fabric.
- Remove all selvages.

press seams

- Use a steam iron on the cotton setting.
- Press the seam just as it was sewn right sides together. This "sets" the seam.
- With dark fabric on top, lift the dark fabric and press back.
- The seam allowance is pressed toward the dark side. Some patterns may direct otherwise for certain situations.
- Follow pressing arrows in the diagrams when indicated.
- Press toward borders. Pieced borders may demand otherwise.
- Press diagonal seams open on binding to reduce bulk.

borders

- Always measure the quilt top 3 times before cutting borders.
- Start measuring about 4" in from each side and through the center vertically.
- Take the average of those 3 measurements.
- Cut 2 border strips to that size. Piece strips together if needed.
- Attach one to either side of the quilt.

- Position the border fabric on top as you sew. The feed dogs can act like rufflers. Having the border on top will prevent waviness and keep the quilt straight.
- Repeat this process for the top and bottom borders, measuring the width 3 times.
- Include the newly attached side borders in your measurements.
- Press toward the borders.

binding

find a video tutorial at: www.msqc.co/006

- Use 2½" strips for binding.
- Sew strips end-to-end into one long strip with diagonal seams, aka the plus sign method (next). Press seams open.
- Fold in half lengthwise wrong sides together and press.
- The entire length should equal the outside dimension of the quilt plus 15" - 20."

plus sign method

- Lay one strip across the other as if to make a plus sign right sides together.
- Sew from top inside to bottom outside corners crossing the intersections of fabric as you sew.
  Trim excess to ¼" seam allowance.
- Press seam open.

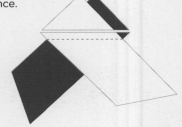

find a video tutorial at: www.msqc.co/001

attach binding

- Match raw edges of folded binding to the quilt top edge.
- Leave a 10" tail at the beginning.
- Use a ¼" seam allowance.
- Start in the middle of a long straight side.

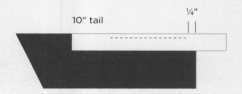

10" tail   ¼"

miter corners

- Stop sewing ¼" before the corner.
- Move the quilt out from under the presser foot.
- Clip the threads.
- Flip the binding up at a 90˚ angle to the edge just sewn.
- Fold the binding down along the next side to be sewn, aligning raw edges.
- The fold will lie along the edge just completed.
- Begin sewing on the fold.

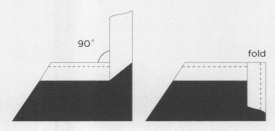

90˚   fold

close binding

MSQC recommends The Binding Tool from TQM Products to finish binding perfectly every time.

- Stop sewing when you have 12" left to reach the start.
- Where the binding tails come together, trim excess leaving only 2½" of overlap.
- It helps to pin or clip the quilt together at the two points where the binding starts and stops. This takes the pressure off of the binding tails while you work.
- Use the plus sign method to sew the two binding ends together, except this time when making the plus sign, match the edges. Using a pencil, mark your sewing line because you won't be able to see where the corners intersect. Sew across.

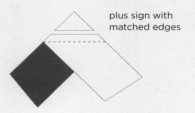

plus sign with
matched edges

- Trim off excess; press seam open.
- Fold in half wrong sides together, and align all raw edges to the quilt top.
- Sew this last binding section to the quilt. Press.
- Turn the folded edge of the binding around to the back of the quilt and tack into place with an invisible stitch or machine stitch if you wish.